D1461920

THE
CORONATION
BOOK OF
QUEEN ELIZABETH II

HER MAJESTY QUEEN ELIZABETH II

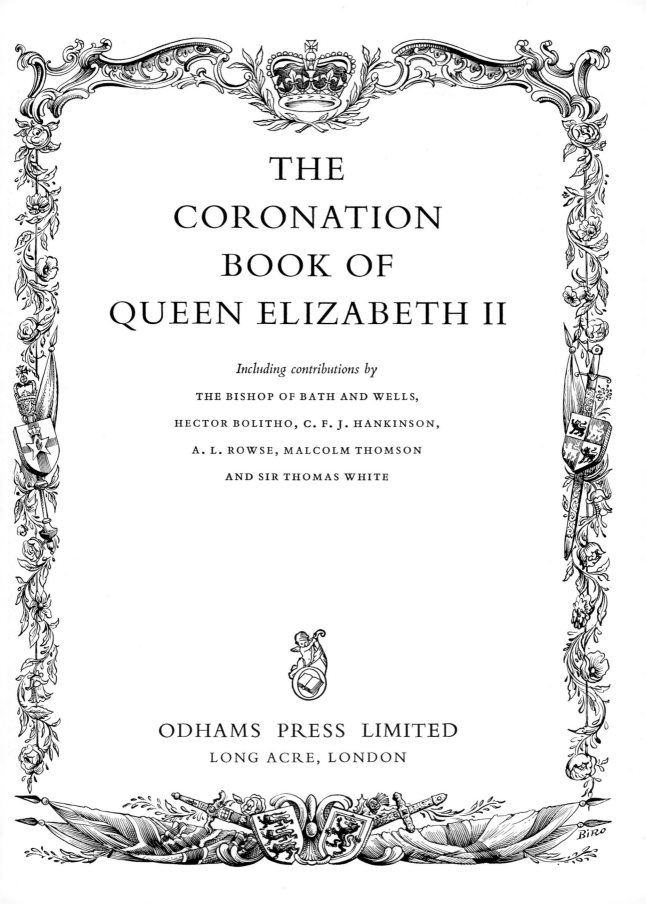

THE CORONATION BOOK OF QUEEN ELIZABETH II

Including contributions by

THE BISHOP OF BATH AND WELLS,

HECTOR BOLITHO, C. F. J. HANKINSON,

A. L. ROWSE, MALCOLM THOMSON

AND SIR THOMAS WHITE

ODHAMS PRESS LIMITED

LONG ACRE, LONDON

The Queen's Dedication

THERE is a motto which has been borne by many of my ancestors—a noble motto, "I serve." Those words were an inspiration to many bygone heirs to the throne when they made their knightly dedication as they came to manhood. I cannot do quite as they did, but through the inventions of science I can do what was not possible for any of them. I can make my solemn act of dedication with a whole Empire listening. I should like to make that dedication now. It is very simple. I declare before you all that my whole life, whether it be long or short, shall be devoted to your service and the service of our great Imperial family to which we all belong, but I shall not have strength to carry out this resolution alone unless you join in it with me, as I now invite you to do. I know that your support will be unfailingly given. God help me to make good my vow, and God bless all of you who are willing to share in it.

*From the Queen's twenty-first-
birthday broadcast from Cape Town,
21 April, 1947*

AT my Coronation next June I shall dedicate myself anew to your service. I shall do so in the presence of a great congregation, drawn from every part of the Commonwealth and Empire, while millions outside Westminster Abbey will hear the promises and the prayers being offered up within its walls, and see much of the ancient ceremony in which kings and queens before me have taken part through century upon century. You will be keeping it as a holiday: but I want to ask you all, whatever your religion may be, to pray for me on that day—to pray that God may give me wisdom and strength to carry out the solemn promises I shall be making, and that I may faithfully serve him, and you, all the days of my life.

*From the Queen's
Christmas Day broadcast
from Sandringham, 1952*

Contents

Colour Plates

PROCLAMATION OF THE CORONATION AT THE ROYAL EXCHANGE, LONDON, 1952

6

The Coronation Ceremony

By C. F. J. HANKINSON

THE Coronation ceremony is probably more splendid and emblematic in England than in any other country in the world, and is of great antiquity. Old records refer to the Coronation of Egferth, King of Mercia (one of the seven kingdoms which existed before England became united under one crown) in 785, but probably there were Coronations even farther back in our history. Naturally in the course of centuries the ceremony has undergone some modifications, but in its essential features it has been subjected to comparatively little change.

The most significant part of the service is the anointing, for just as Saul, chosen when the Israelites asked for a king, was anointed by the Prophet Samuel, so also have all our kings been anointed with Holy Oil. The great importance attached to this is perhaps best expressed in the words uttered by Shakespeare's Richard II on the invasion of Bolingbroke:

> *"Not all the water in the rough rude sea*
> *Can wash the balm from an anointed King."*

The anointing oil used at present is prepared from pure olive oil and on the morning of the Coronation is poured into the ampulla, after which it is placed on the high altar and there consecrated by the Archbishop of Canterbury. It is not perhaps without significance that at this supremely important point in the ceremony the only two items of the Coronation regalia which survived destruction at the hands of the Parliamentarians after the Civil War are brought into use—the ampulla and the spoon. These, unlike the other articles of the regalia, are not carried in the Sovereign's procession in the Abbey, but are placed on the altar before the service.

As might be expected there are numerous legends regarding the various objects in the regalia, and it may be of interest to mention that according to one of these the Virgin Mary appeared to St. Thomas à Becket whilst he was on a visit to France, and gave him the ampulla together with holy oil for anointing English kings. For a time the ampulla was lost, but later was found by the Black Prince at Poitiers and brought to England. There it was placed in the Tower of London, but seems again to have been

LEADING FIGURES IN THE CORONATION

The organization of the Coronation is in the hands of the Earl Marshal (*left*); the Archbishop of Canterbury (*centre*), assisted by the Dean of Westminster (*right*), conducts the Service.

overlooked and does not appear to have been discovered until the reign of Richard II. As Richard had been crowned already, it could not be used until the Coronation of his cousin, Henry IV. Another legend relates to the original Coronation ring, which, so the story runs, was given by Edward the Confessor to St. John the Evangelist, who appeared to him disguised as a beggar. Afterwards the ring was given by St. John to two English pilgrims in the Holy Land with instructions to return it to Edward, and to tell him that Divine grace should encircle every English sovereign who was invested with it at his Coronation.

When the Queen reaches Westminster Abbey on the morning of 2 June, a fanfare of trumpets will be sounded to herald her arrival. On alighting from the State Coach in which all our sovereigns have ridden on their way to be crowned since it was built for King George III, the Queen will be received at the West door by the Earl Marshal, the Duke of Norfolk, upon whom rests the responsibility for all the arrangements.

The office of Earl Marshal was created as long ago as 1483 and is hereditary in the family of the Duke of Norfolk. The Duke has a place near the Sovereign throughout the ceremony, sustains the royal crown when necessary, and carries a special baton.

The procession, which had been formed in the annexe by the West door to await the Queen's coming, on her arrival moves into the Abbey in all its brilliance. In it will walk the archbishops and bishops, representatives of the Church of Scotland and of the Free Churches, the Standard Bearers, the Barons of the Cinque Ports, the four Knights of the Garter selected to hold the silken pall over the Queen whilst she is being anointed, the Prime Minister of the United Kingdom, the Prime Ministers of the Dominions, the Heralds and Pursuivants, the peers who carry the regalia, and other great personages, who will proceed with the Queen to the theatre, or specially erected platform, on which the ceremony will take place.

At the Coronation of King George VI the significance of the occasion for the whole British Commonwealth of Nations was emphasized by the carrying in the procession of the standards of Canada, Australia, New Zealand, South Africa and India by the High Commissioners of those countries, in addition to the Union Standard and Quarterings of the Royal Arms, and the Royal Standard. Since then other overseas territories have attained sovereign status, within the Commonwealth, and their representatives will join those of the older Dominions in proudly bearing their standards aloft on this memorable occasion.

The regalia is borne immediately before the Queen—the St. Edward's Staff, the Sceptre with the Cross, the two Golden Spurs, the five Swords of State, the Sceptre with the Dove, and the Orb, each carried by peers attended by one page, the St. Edward's Crown, borne on a velvet cushion by the Lord High Steward attended by two pages, and the Chalice and Paten and the Bible by three Bishops. In this part of the procession will also walk the Kings of Arms carrying their crowns, the Gentleman Usher of the Black Rod, and the Lord Mayor of London with the City mace.

THE ABBEY ANNEXE
For the last five Coronations a temporary annexe has been built adjoining Westminster Abbey. It provides robing and retiring rooms and a space in which the processions can be organized before entering the Abbey. This picture shows a scale model of the annexe designed for the Coronation of Queen Elizabeth II.

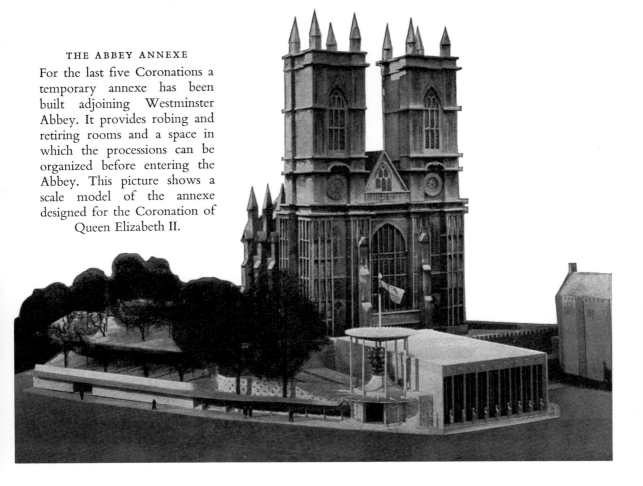

THE REGALIA READY FOR THE CORONATION

Before the ceremony the Regalia, after being brought from the Jewel House at the Tower of London, rests on a special table in the Abbey annexe. (This picture was taken in 1937.)

The Lord High Steward, whose great privilege it is to bear the crown, should not be confused with the Lord Steward of the Household, who is a permanent official. He holds an office of great antiquity, which was established prior to the reign of Edward the Confessor. In those days the heir to the Throne was not considered to be king until he had been anointed and crowned, and in the interval between the death of one sovereign and the crowning of his successor the Lord High Steward acted as Viceroy. Since the time of Henry IV the office has been merged in the Crown, as it was then considered to be too powerful to be safely entrusted to any subject. The appointment, however, is revived on certain important occasions for the carrying out of some special duties on the completion of which the commission of appointment expires. Another Great Officer of State who has a place in the procession and who is appointed for the occasion only is the Lord High Constable of England, who walks with the Earl Marshal and during the ceremony stands at the left of the Sovereign.

When at last the young Queen herself comes into view of the vast and eagerly expectant congregation, the forty Queen's Scholars of Westminster School will hail her with shouts of "*Vivat Regina Elizabetha. Vivat! Vivat! Vivat!*" These fortunate boys of the school adjoining the Abbey have had for centuries past the highly prized right of attending Coronations and hailing the new sovereign in the only Latin words now used in the service; the school was founded by Queen Elizabeth I. When the procession reaches the theatre the Queen, after kneeling for a private prayer, will take

10

her seat in the Chair of State. The Archbishop of Canterbury, together with the Lord Chancellor, the Lord Great Chamberlain (whose office is hereditary and not to be confused with that of the Lord Chamberlain, who is a permanent official and head of the Sovereign's Household), the Lord High Constable, and the Earl Marshal, Garter King of Arms preceding them, will go in turn to the four corners of the theatre and recite the recognition at each, turning east, south, west, and north. Meanwhile the Sovereign, standing by her Chair, will turn and show herself to the people at each side. The form of recognition used is: "Sirs, I here present unto you Queen Elizabeth, your undoubted Queen: Wherefore all you who are come this day to do your homage and service, are you willing to do the same?" The people will signify their willingness and cry out: "God Save Queen Elizabeth," and the trumpets will sound. This part of the service is a survival of the days when the sovereign about to be crowned was not always the undisputed successor to the Throne, and the acceptance of the Queen by the people will show that she reigns by their will.

The Bible, chalice and paten are now placed on the altar by the bishops who bore them in the procession, and the peers who carried the regalia, except the swords, deliver them up so that they also may be placed upon the altar. The next part of the ceremony is the administration of the Oath. The Archbishop comes to the Queen and, standing before her, says: "Madam, is your Majesty willing to take the Oath?" and the Queen will reply: "I am willing." The Queen will then solemnly promise and swear to govern the peoples of the United Kingdom, each of the Dominions, which she will name separately, and her Provinces and other Territories according to their respective laws and customs. She will also promise to the utmost of her power to maintain in the United Kingdom the Protestant Reformed Religion established by law. Then arising from her chair, with the Sword of State carried before her, she will go to the altar, where she will take the Oath in the sight of all the people, laying her right hand upon the Bible which was carried in the procession, saying:

CORONATION OF GEORGE V
The Regalia, Chalice and Paten, and Bible being carried into the Abbey.

11

"The things which I have here before promised I will perform, and keep. So help me God." She will then kiss the book and sign the Oath.

After prayers, readings from the Bible by two of the bishops, and the singing of the Creed and a hymn, the Queen will be anointed. For this part of the service she will be divested of her crimson robe by the Lord Great Chamberlain and will then sit in King Edward's Chair. The chair was made by order of King Edward I to hold the Coronation Stone, or Stone of Destiny, on which the Scottish kings used to sit when they were crowned. The stone was brought to Westminster in 1296 after being captured by King Edward, and has remained there ever since except for a brief period after it was stolen on Christmas Day, 1950. With the possible exception of Queen Mary I, who is said to have been crowned in a chair specially sent for her by the Pope, all our sovereigns commencing with Edward II have sat in this chair at their Coronations.

During the anointing four Knights of the Garter will hold over the Queen a rich pall of silk, or cloth of gold, and the Dean of Westminster will take from the altar the ampulla and spoon, pouring some of the holy oil into the spoon and holding it whilst the Archbishop anoints Her Majesty in the form of a cross, saying, "Be thou anointed with Holy Oil as Kings, Priests and Prophets were anointed." The Queen will then kneel at her faldstool and the Archbishop will say a blessing over her. She will then resume her seat in King Edward's Chair and the Knights of the Garter will give back the pall to the Lord Chamberlain. Then the Queen will arise to enable the Dean of Westminster to put on her vestments: first the *Colobium Sindonis*, a surplice without sleeves and made of very fine white linen and an ancient dress of bishops and priests, and then the *Supertunica*, which is a long close coat with wide sleeves made entirely of cloth of gold and embroidered in an ecclesiastical design. The Queen will then resume her seat, and will be presented with the Spurs by the Lord Great Chamberlain, who has received them

from the Dean of Westminster. They will then be returned to the altar.

Next, the peer who has carried the Sword of State in the procession delivers it to the Lord Great Chamberlain (whereupon it is deposited in the traverse in St. Edward's Chapel), and receives from him in lieu there-

STATE TRUMPET
The State trumpets, made of solid silver, sound a fanfare following the act of crowning.

12

of another sword in a scabbard of purple velvet which he delivers to the Archbishop, who lays it on the altar with a prayer. The Archbishop then takes the sword from the altar and places it in the Queen's right hand and the Queen holds it while the Archbishop says: "Receive this Kingly sword brought now from the altar of God and delivered to you by the hands of us the bishops and servants of God though unworthy."

Had the Sovereign been a king the sword would then have been girt about him by the Lord Great Chamberlain, but if the precedent of Queen Victoria's Coronation is followed the sword will not be girded about the Queen but will be placed by her on the altar and the peer who carried the Great Sword of State in the procession will offer the price of one hundred shillings to redeem it. The Dean of Westminster will then take the sword from

KING EDWARD'S CHAIR

Beneath the seat is the Coronation Stone, with a history dating back to the year 850, when it was placed in the Abbey of Scone.

the altar and hand it to the peer, who will draw it out of its scabbard and carry it naked before Her Majesty during the remainder of the service.

Then follows the investing with the armills (bracelets), the stole royal and the robe royal. The stole royal is of cloth of gold lined with rose-coloured silk with fringed ends, and having worked on it various emblems representative of the Commonwealth and a cross of St. George at each end. The robe royal is like a cope and is lined with Indian red satin, and embroidered with laurel leaves and emblems of the countries comprising the United Kingdom. When these have been put on the Queen by the Dean of Westminster, to whom they will be delivered by the Groom of the Robes, the Lord Great Chamberlain fastening the clasps, the Queen will sit and the orb will be brought from the altar by the Dean of Westminster and placed in her hand with an exhortation in which she will be reminded that the orb which signifies Imperial power is surmounted by the Cross to indicate that the whole world is subject to the power and Empire of Christ our Redeemer. The Queen will then hand back the orb to the Dean of Westminster, who will replace it on the altar.

13

PRINCIPAL FEATURES OF THE CORONATION CEREMONY

The photographs on these pages (taken at the Coronation of King George VI in 1937) illustrate many of the rites (described in the accompanying article) which will be repeated at the Coronation of Queen Elizabeth II with minor variations to adapt the procedure to the Coronation of a Queen. The first picture (*reading from left to right above*) shows the Sovereign facing the people during the Recognition. The second picture shows the Anointing. The Sovereign has taken off the Robe and Cap of State, and is seated on King Edward's Chair under a cloth of gold. This is carried by four Knights of the Garter who have been summoned by Garter King of Arms. The third and fourth pictures show the King holding the orb and the two

FROM THE RECOGNITION TO THE HOMAGE

sceptres while the Archbishop of Canterbury takes St. Edward's Crown from the Dean of Westminster in preparation for the crowning. In the picture below (*left*) the actual crowning is about to take place; the last picture shows the Homage. In this the Sovereign has left St. Edward's Chair and is seated on the throne; all the peers are wearing their coronets. On either side of the Sovereign are the Bishops of Durham and Bath and Wells and the words of the homage are led by the Archbishop of Canterbury kneeling before the throne. The other bishops kneel in their places. The Duke of Edinburgh and the Royal Dukes pay their homage individually, but the Orders of the Peerage follow a procedure similar to that of the bishops.

The Keeper of the Jewel House will then hand the Queen's ring to the Archbishop who will put it on the fourth finger of her right hand. The Sceptre with the Cross and the Sceptre with the Dove will also be handed to the Archbishop, and a glove having been presented to the Queen, the Archbishop will place the Sceptre with the Cross in the Queen's right hand, saying: "Receive the Royal Sceptre, the ensign of Kingly power and justice," and the Sceptre with the Dove in her left hand with an exhortation to punish the wicked and protect the just. With this concluded there follows the supreme moment which all have been awaiting—the crowning.

The Archbishop will take the St. Edward's Crown from the altar and, accompanied by other bishops, and the Dean of Westminster carrying the Crown, will go to the Queen and place it on her head. The people will then shout "God Save the Queen," the peers, peeresses, and Kings of Arms will put on their coronets, the trumpets will sound, and by a given signal the guns at the Tower will be fired.

The Archbishop will next present the Queen with the Bible and she will return it to him to be replaced on the altar. He will then solemnly bless her and pronounce a benediction. After this the Queen will go to her throne and be lifted up into it by the Archbishop and bishops and other peers, and the Great Officers of State will stand round her whilst the Archbishop delivers an exhortation.

The scene is now set for the Homage. First of all the Archbishop of Canterbury, kneeling before the throne, will lead the bishops, who remain kneeling in their places, in uttering their promise to be faithful and true to Her Majesty and will kiss the Queen's right hand; then the Duke of Edinburgh, Duke of Gloucester and Duke of Kent will do homage individually and will kiss the Queen's left cheek, and the senior of each of the other degrees of the Peerage, on behalf of the others of their rank, will also do homage. When the Homage is completed the drums will be beaten and the trumpets will be sounded and the people will shout: "God Save Queen Elizabeth. Long Live Queen Elizabeth. May the Queen live for ever."

The Communion Service will follow, after which the Queen will go to St. Edward's Chapel, where the Sceptre with the Dove, the Spurs and St. Edward's Staff will be given up to the Dean of Westminster, who will lay them on the altar. The Queen will then be disrobed of her robe royal and arrayed in her robe of purple velvet, and having put on the Imperial Crown in place of the St. Edward's Crown she will proceed at the head of the re-formed procession of those who accompanied her on her entry into the Abbey, to the West door, where she will take her place in the State Coach and set out on the return journey to Buckingham Palace.

PORTRAIT, 1951

ENGAGEMENT GROUP, BUCKINGHAM PALACE, 1947

FAMILY PORTRAIT, 1951

THE REGALIA

The items of the Regalia described here will feature prominently in the Coronation Ceremony:

The Orb (1) is the Emblem of sovereignty and is a ball of gold six inches across circled by a gold band decorated with diamonds and edged with pearls. Above the ball, set on an amethyst, is a cross studded with diamonds, with a sapphire in the middle on one side and an emerald on the other.

The St. Edward's Crown (2) is the official Crown of England and the one with which the Sovereign is usually crowned. It is of gold set with pearls and precious stones and has two complete arches crossing each other. At the meeting point of these is a mound with a cross on it. The cap within the framework is of crimson velvet turned up with ermine.

The Imperial Crown of State (3) is worn at the end of the Coronation Ceremony and also on State occasions such as the Opening of Parliament. It was made for the Coronation of Queen Victoria. Amongst the priceless jewels with which it is set are the famous Black Prince's ruby which is said to have been given to him by King Pedro of Castile in 1367, and to have been worn in the Crown Helmet of Henry V at the Battle of Agincourt; the great Stuart sapphire from the Crown of Charles II, bequeathed by Henry, Cardinal York, to George III; a sapphire stated to have been taken from the Coronation Ring of Edward the Confessor; the smaller of the two greater portions of the "Star of Africa" diamond, presented by Transvaal to Edward VII; and the pearls which according to tradition were taken from ear-rings belonging to Queen Elizabeth I.

The Sword of State (4) is a large two-handed sword with a scabbard of crimson velvet decorated with gold plates of the Royal Badge and having one side of the guard fashioned as a lion and the other as a unicorn.

The Sword of Mercy, of Curtana, is the shortest of the three swords (5, 6 and 7) and is pointless. The other two swords are the Sword of Spiritual Justice, which has a handle covered with fine gold wire, a pommel of plain steel gilt and a scabbard covered with crimson velvet, and the Sword of Temporal Justice which is similar.

The Jewelled Sword (8), which is girt about the Sovereign at the Coronations of Kings, is richly decorated with precious stones in a design incorporating the national emblems of England, Scotland and Ireland.

The Ampulla (9), which is a gold flask containing the Holy Oil for anointing, is in the form of an eagle with wings outspread standing on a pedestal. The head unscrews to enable the oil to be poured in. The Spoon is of silver gilt with four pearls set in the handle.

The Spurs (10) are of a pattern worn by Anglo-Saxons and Normans and have no rowels, but end in an ornamental point. The Coronation Ring is of gold set with a large ruby, on which a cross of St. George is enchased. It is jointed like a bracelet.

The Royal Sceptre (11) is of gold and is two feet nine inches in length. At the top is the great amethyst set in the form of an orb, over which is a cross thickly studded with diamonds. Just under the orb is set the larger of the two greater portions of the "Star of Africa" diamond.

St. Edward's Staff (12) is another sceptre which is much longer than the Royal Sceptre. It has at the end a steel tip and was probably originally used as a walking stick.

The Sceptre with the Dove (13), sometimes called the Virge, is similar to the Royal Sceptre, except that it has a white enamelled dove at the top instead of a cross.

WESTMINSTER ABBEY: THE CORONATION CHURCH

18

The Significance of
the Coronation

By THE BISHOP OF BATH AND WELLS

THE Coronation from a constitutional point of view adds nothing to the Queen which she does not already possess. According to English law, the Sovereign assumes the Throne from the very moment that it is vacated. Her Proclamation is the announcement of an accomplished fact. What then is the significance of the Coronation? The answer to this question is written throughout the closely intertwined history of Church and State since Saxon times. There is something more in the conception of sovereignty than an office of State, and it derives from the fact that the English constitution rests firmly upon the Christian faith and tradition. It is a vocation to a sacred office which demands not only popular acclaim, and constitutional sanction, but also the outward and visible signs of a Divine call, of the grace and favour of God, and of a personal dedication to the service of God, and to the service of the peoples throughout the British Commonwealth over whom the Queen reigns.

The rite of the Coronation is hallowed by centuries of tradition, and remains essentially unchanged, though its history inevitably reflects changes in the constitution of the British nation and Commonwealth. It is, as it always has been, embedded in the Holy Communion Service of the Church of England, and is therefore a unique solemnity and pageantry in the partnership of Church and State. Its significance must be measured in terms of spiritual values, and not in terms of outward pageantry and show, except in so far as these outward forms are sacramental in character, and point to spiritual truths and factors of immense importance in the office of the Sovereign, and in the personal and corporate lives of those over whom she reigns. There is real danger in so great a concentration upon the material setting of the Coronation, with all its splendour, that its essential significance remains unrealized. A brief glance at the principal features of the Coronation Service will reveal both its intensely religious character and the spiritual principles which underlie it.

First there is an elective element in the recognition and the acclamation of the Sovereign, who is anointed and crowned in response to the will and choice of the

19

people. This goes back to Anglo-Saxon times, long before the hereditary principle was finally established at the Coronation of Edward I. The Queen is presented to her people by the Archbishop of Canterbury and high officers of State, as their undoubted Sovereign whose office demands both the homage and service of her subjects. From the moment of the recognition, the Queen's dedication of herself to the service of God and of her people presupposes a similar dedication on the part of all her subjects.

Once the Queen has been presented and acclaimed the Oath is administered, whereby a contractual obligation is ratified, through which Her Majesty undertakes first to govern all her peoples, and to administer law and justice, in mercy, and second to maintain unimpaired the faith and worship of the Church of England from which she derives her spiritual authority. The changing character of the Oath throughout the ages is an epitome of English constitutional history, but its inner and spiritual significance is unimpaired. It is a binding contract in terms of spiritual and moral values between the Queen and her peoples.

The Queen's anointing constitutes the essence of the ceremony, for the use of holy oil is hallowed by centuries of Christian tradition as the mark of consecration. Though we refer to the whole ceremony as that of the Coronation, it is in effect the consecration of the Queen to her office of which the anointing is the outward and visible sign. The delivery of the regalia, and indeed the putting on of the crown itself, are adjuncts, and interpretations of the mystery of sacring or hallowing, whereby Divine approval of the people's will is bestowed, and also grace for the fulfilment of the task. By the anointing and the delivery of the regalia the Queen is habited as a spiritual person having not only a temporal authority but a spiritual sanction. The Sovereign is in a sense God's overseer both of Church and realm. It is significant that the regalia, sword, robe, ring, orb, sceptre and the crown itself are delivered by the principal spiritual persons present, thereby symbolizing the dependence of the Sovereign upon the Church of Christ for confirmation in her office, for her consecration as a minister of God in Church and State, and for Divine grace to sustain and support her.

There remains one further principal element in this intense spiritual drama. When all the symbols of spiritual and temporal authority have been bestowed, there remains the Queen's own spiritual need both to dedicate herself to her task, and to acknowledge her own inability for it, apart from the grace of God. So in a real sense the climax of the whole rite for her is in the act of Communion, wherein she offers "herself, her soul and body to be a reasonable, holy and living sacrifice" and she receives the sacramental gift through which her soul and body are preserved unto everlasting life. Please God,

QUEEN VICTORIA TAKING THE SACRAMENT AT HER CORONATION

Queen Victoria is kneeling before the Altar receiving the sacrament from the Archbishop of
Canterbury; in the right foreground is the Duke of Wellington. (From a contemporary print.)

many will share with her that simple but profound sacrament of grace and fellowship.

It is clear from a study of the rite that the Coronation is in no sense an act affecting
the Queen in isolation from her people, but if its full significance is to be realized her
subjects must take their own full share in it, not merely as spectators, but as her faithful
lieges dedicating themselves with her to the service of God in Church and State. Behind
all the pageantry and splendour lies the tremendous fact that God still calls his creatures
into partnership with Himself, and that we are His fellow workers in the fulfilment of
His will and purpose.

21

QUEEN ELIZABETH I WITH THE REGALIA: FROM AN ENGRAVING DATED 1596

22

Coronations in English History

By A. L. ROWSE

THE English monarchy is the oldest of our political institutions—many centuries older than Parliament—and except for the Papacy, the oldest in Europe. The Coronation ceremony goes back with the monarchy to the early days of the Anglo-Saxon kings. The earliest recension of the service we have is from the eighth century: it already contains the essential elements—the anointing of the king, the delivery of the emblems of power, rod, sceptre, helmet, and the enthronement. We know that when King Edgar was crowned on Whit Sunday, 973, by St. Dunstan, care was taken to get the exact form of the service right. It is fascinating to think that the ceremony has remained in essence the same for over a thousand years: a thing to be proud of in a world without much sense of order or of the past. Thank goodness the English are in this, as in some other things, an exception!

When William the Conqueror had defeated Harold at Hastings and entered London, he wished to postpone his Coronation till his wife could join him. But it was urgent that the ceremony should take place to secure his position: he would not be really king until he was anointed and crowned. So on Christmas day, 1066, the ceremony took place in Edward the Confessor's Abbey at Westminster. The Conqueror swore the oath to rule his people justly. When he was presented to the people for their acknowledgement as king, the question was put to them both in English and in French. The shout of assent was misunderstood by William's followers outside: thinking that their leader was in danger, they set about them. People rushed out of the Abbey, the surrounding buildings were fired; William, quivering with excitement, was left almost alone with the clergy to complete the ceremony. His self-control was rewarded: his Coronation placed him firmly in the succession of the old English kings.

The Coronation of Richard Coeur-de-Lion, 3 September, 1189, is memorable as that on which the service reached the full development at which it became fixed for the future. Richard was acclaimed by the people, took the threefold oath to maintain the peace of the Church, suppress injustice and promote equity and mercy. He then received the threefold anointing. Adjured by the Archbishop not to assume the crown unless he intended to keep his vow, he answered that by God's help he did. When,

CORONATION PROCESSION OF EDWARD VI, 1547

Until the time of James II it was the custom for the Sovereign to go in procession from the Tower of London, then a royal residence, to Westminster on the day before the Coronation. The old print reproduced here shows Edward VI's procession passing along Cheapside.

ten years later, Richard's brother John was crowned, he deliberately abstained from communicating: he did not mean to over-exert himself in observing the oaths he took.

Mary Tudor was the first reigning queen to be crowned; and after the breach in ritual made by the Reformation, she had to send abroad to the Emperor's Chancellor, who was a bishop, for the chrism for her anointing. The traditional procession from the Tower to Westminster took place, with pageants all the way, on 30 September, 1553. Next day, since Archbishop Cranmer was in prison, Gardiner, Bishop of Winchester, crowned the Queen; the Princess Elizabeth and Anne of Cleves, arrayed in crimson, coronets on their heads, stood behind her. On her way back Elizabeth complained of the weight of her coronet; her friend, the French ambassador, replied: "Have patience: it is only the preliminary to one that will sit more lightly."

Elizabeth I's own Coronation five years later, 15 January, 1559, was the last to take place with the Latin service of Plantagenet times. The traditional ceremonies were observed in full: the procession from the Tower on the eve of the Coronation, that from Westminster Hall to the Abbey on the day, the Coronation itself and the return to Westminster Hall for the banquet. The religious changes she intended to make were already foreshadowed and the Queen was faced with passive resistance on the part of Mary's Catholic bishops. At last one of them, Oglethorpe, Bishop of Carlisle, was prevailed on to crown her; but while he proceeded to the elevation of the Host at the Mass, the Queen withdrew to her traverse or private pew. Nor did she lie prostrate on the floor while *Veni Creator* and the Litany were sung; she knelt before the altar, and "leaned upon the cushions" for her anointing. She was supported, not by the bishops of Durham and of Bath and Wells, as the tradition was and is, but by the earls of Shrewsbury and Pembroke. I am sure that that did not bother her: she would much prefer the proximity of two good-looking earls to a couple of ill-favoured bishops. The latter were put in their place, when it came to doing homage to the Queen, by making them take their places after the temporal peers; nor did they receive their customary allowance of scarlet—only Oglethorpe did, who had earned it. The total effect was to enhance the temporal side of Elizabeth's Coronation, to which she was not averse. Though, some years after, when it suited her, she told the French ambassador that she had been crowned and anointed according to the ceremonies of the Catholic Church and by Catholic bishops, without assisting all through the Mass.

In all other respects the traditional ceremonies were followed; and an Italian report says that, carrying her sceptre and orb, "she returned very cheerfully with a most smiling countenance for every one, giving them all a thousand greetings, so that in my opinion she exceeded the bounds of gravity and decorum." Playing to the gallery, as usual, which no one did to more point or with greater success.

For the Coronation of James I the service was translated for the first time into English, and the Communion service took the place of Mass; otherwise the traditional forms were observed. So, too, for his son, Charles I; though his wife, Henrietta Maria— no more than a girl, but already displaying

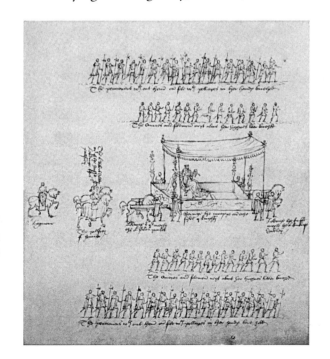

ELIZABETH I'S CORONATION PROCESSION
A contemporary sketch, probably made by one of the heralds, of the Queen's litter with its attendants and escort passing through London.

25

that temper which made her such a fatal influence—refused to attend the ceremony. From a window in Westminster she watched her husband go by, clad all in white, under the dark, lowering skies. Some who witnessed the last scene in Whitehall, under similar dark skies on 30 January, 1649, recalled that white was the colour of martyrs.

Charles II's Coronation was a much jollier affair, after the horrid experience of civil war and the dismal rule of the saints. Dear Pepys, of course, was there: "up early, and made myself as fine as I could, and put on my velvet coat, the first day that I put it on, though made half a year ago"—to see the King's procession from the Tower to Whitehall. Next day, 23 April, 1661, he rose about four and got to the Abbey, "and with much ado did get up into a great scaffold across the north end of the Abbey, where with a great deal of patience I sat from past four till eleven before the King come in." All was very magnificent, the restored bishops in cloth-of-gold copes, even the very fiddlers in red vests. Pepys' breast swelled with loyalty and pleasure; but when it came to the actual Coronation "to my great grief I and most in the Abbey could not see."

However, Pepys made up for it by enjoying the spectacle in Westminster Hall, the three peers on horseback, the King's champion all in armour, the challenges and the dining and wining. "I took a great deal of pleasure to go up and down, and look upon the ladies, and to hear the musique of all sorts, but above all, the 24 violins." Afterwards he went a-drinking the King's health in Whitehall, "and I wondered to see how the ladies did tipple." Mr. Pepys retired to bed that night exhausted; "but no sooner a-bed with Mr. Shepley but my head began to turn, and I to vomitt, and if ever I was foxed, it was now."

James II, being a Catholic, had the Communion service omitted and ordered Archbishop Sancroft to abridge the excessive length of the rest. Which was done. But James as his cleverer brother had foretold, lasted no longer than three years. The Revolution of 1688 brought in William and Mary as joint sovereigns; and their Coronation—in the conservative manner of English revolutions—went back to the traditional order of encasing the Coronation in the Communion service. This is the form that the ceremony has essentially followed ever since. There is nothing special to remark about Queen Anne's Coronation, 23 April, 1702; except that the Queen, already afflicted with gout and unable to endure even a short procession to the Abbey, "had the conveniency to be carried in a low open chair," and this had the advantage that she was seen by all.

When we come to George III's Coronation, in 1761, we have the whole thing described by the brilliant and slightly barbed pen of Horace Walpole. He was, as usual,

STUART CORONATIONS

When Charles I was executed his elder son hurried from France to Scotland, where he was crowned Charles II at Scone (a contemporary print of the event is reproduced on the right). Charles had to wait until 1661 and the restoration of the monarchy in England for his Coronation at Westminster. Charles was succeeded by his brother, James II, whose Coronation with that of his Queen, Mary of Modena, is illustrated in the print reproduced below. The principal participants in the ceremony are identified and occupy the same positions as their successors in office will occupy for the Coronation of Queen Elizabeth II in June, 1953.

everywhere, peeping into everything, taking a hand in everything, helping one peeress to dress her hair, undressing other peeresses' reputations, and writing it all down to amuse his friends. "Oh! the buzz, the prattle, the crowds, the noise, the hurry! If I was to entitle ages, I would call this the *century of crowds.* . . . What is the finest sight in the world? A Coronation. What do people talk most about? A Coronation. What is delightful to have passed? A Coronation. Indeed, one had need to be a handsome young peeress not to be fatigued to death with it." But even Horace Walpole, like others who have come to be bored, could not help being impressed. "The multitudes, balconies, guards and processions made Palace Yard the liveliest spectacle in the world; the Hall was the most glorious."

But in a circle like Walpole's everything has to be made fun of, and there were plenty of incidents. At the Coronation banquet, "Lord Talbot piqued himself on backing his horse down the Hall and not turning its rump towards the King; but he had taken such pains to dress it to that duty that it entered backwards; and at his retreat the

A JOINT CORONATION

The Coronation of William III and Mary II in 1689 is unique in British history as a joint Coronation of husband and wife as reigning sovereigns. In consequence, additional items of regalia known as the Queen's orb and the Queen's sceptre had to be specially made.

spectators clapped, a terrible indecorum, but suitable to such Bartholomew Fair doings." The Duke of Newcastle was always a comic turn on these occasions. And in the Abbey, "of all the incidents of the day, the most diverting was what happened to the Queen. She had a retiring chamber, with *all* conveniences, prepared behind the altar. She went thither—in the *most convenient* what found she but—the Duke of Newcastle!" The bishops were ill-rehearsed in their parts; so that when it came to the Communion no one could tell the King whether he should take his crown off or keep it on. The King asked the Archbishop, who couldn't answer, and asked the Bishop of Rochester, who

QUEEN ANNE

Queen Anne is the only British queen prior to Queen Elizabeth II to have had a consort at the time of her Coronation.

didn't know. The King, very properly, took the crown off. The Earl Marshal confessed that "there had been great neglect in that office, but he had now taken such care of registering directions that the *next Coronation* would be conducted with the greatest order imaginable."

It could hardly be said to have been; for it was that of George IV and he had a terrible problem on his hands—his wife, Queen Caroline, from whom he had been living apart for years and who now specially returned from abroad to "claim her rights," aided by the London mob: in short, to make trouble. George IV, already sufficiently unpopular and driven to distraction by her, and several other little things, was in despair at this hefty apparition bearing down on him just at this moment. He besought the Marquis Wellesley to come to breakfast at Carlton House: "Come on *foot* and enter through the *stables* by the gate where the sentinels are, the *nearest* to Spring Garden Passage. *I want your private advice and support,* as an *old and attached friend,* and there is *much* to be communicated to *you.*" One sees that heavy underlining did not enter the Royal Family's epistolary style with Queen Victoria.

George IV was a good comic turn—though serious-minded people thought him rather more than a joke; everything conspired to make him ridiculous. The intolerable Caroline announced her intention of being present—in spite of all the scandal the so-called "delicate investigation" into her conduct abroad had caused, and the slump

29

in her popularity with the mob. She sent a message to say that she would be at the Abbey at 8 a.m.; but she arrived between 6 and 7 a.m. to take people by surprise. She did not succeed: she tried every door and found her entry barred. Hissed in the streets and overwhelmed by humiliation, she died a month after, to everybody's relief. While George IV, with the crown safely on his head, went off on a Coronation tour and a rapturous reception in Ireland, where he may be said to have been in his element.

Queen Victoria's Coronation, only eighteen years later, was not without a certain Regency flavour. There was the aristocratic, Whiggish Greville looking on (28 June, 1838), and writing it all down in his Diary in his condescending, subacid way. "The different actors in the ceremonial were very imperfect in their parts, and had neglected to rehearse them. Nobody knew what was to be done except the Archbishop and Lord John Thynne (who had rehearsed), Lord Willoughby (who is experienced in these matters) and the Duke of Wellington, and consequently there was a continual difficulty and embarrassment, and the Queen never knew what she was to do next. They made her leave her chair and enter into St. Edward's chapel before the prayers were concluded, much to the discomfiture of the Archbishop. She said to John Thynne, 'Pray tell me what I am to do, for they don't know'; and at the end, when the orb was put into her hand, she said to him, 'What am I to do with it?' 'Your Majesty is to carry it, if you please, in your hand.' 'Am I?' she said; 'it is very heavy.' The ruby ring was made for her little finger instead of the fourth, on which the rubric prescribes that it should be put. When the Archbishop was to put it on, she extended the former, but he said it must be on the latter. She said it was too small, and she could not get it on. As he insisted, she yielded, but had first to take off her other rings, and then this was forced on, but it hurt her very much."

There was another *contretemps* when old Lord Rolle, nearly ninety, coming up to do homage rolled down the steps instead. The old boy made a gallant second try, and this time the Queen rose from the throne and went down a step or two to help him. This good sense and kindness on her part made a very favourable impression. In fact, Greville, in spite of finding everything very tiresome and yet going everywhere like Horace Walpole, could not help, any less than Horace, being impressed. That evening he met Prince Esterhazy and asked him what the foreign representatives were saying. Esterhazy replied that they all admired it very much: "Strogonoff (the Russian envoy) and the others don't like you, but they feel it, and it makes a great impression on them; in fact, nothing can be seen like it in any other country." How recurrent—almost repetitive—are the themes of history!

30

THE FIRST OF THE HANOVERIANS

George I, great-grandson of James I, was Elector of Hanover when he succeeded Queen
Anne in 1714. In this painting from Kneller's studio, he is depicted in the robes of the Order
of the Garter, with St. Edward's Crown, the orb and sceptre on the table beside him.

31

It seems that a Coronation is one of the things that we do better in this century; certainly more forethought and preparation are given to it, the whole thing more carefully rehearsed. Edward VII, who had a taste for opulent pageantry, planned his on a splendid scale; the heirs of all the European sovereigns—who then existed in some number—were to be there. At the last moment the King fell ill and the Coronation had to be postponed. When it took place on 9 August, 1902, it bore more the character of a family event, with the Commonwealth very much to the fore. The whole thing is described by Sir Sidney Lee, in the breathless style he thought proper to the occasion: "within the Abbey all was hushed and expectant," "the Queen passed gracefully to her seat," etc.

The description of his own Coronation by Edward's sailor son, George V, with its nautical observations on the weather, has a simpler, homelier note and reveals a charming good nature. "*Thursday, June 22nd*, 1911. *Our Coronation Day. Buckingham Palace.* It was overcast and cloudy with some showers and a strongish cool breeze, but better for the people than great heat. Today was indeed a great and memorable day in our lives and one we can never forget, but it brought back to me many sad memories of nine years ago, when the beloved Parents were crowned. . . . The service in the Abbey was most beautiful, but it was a terrible ordeal. It was grand, yet simple and dignified and went without a hitch. I nearly broke down when dear David came to do homage to me, as it

CORONATION PROCESSION OF WILLIAM IV

Unlike present-day practice, this old print of the State Coach approaching the Abbey shows a coachman on the box with postillions provided for the first three pairs of horses only.

CORONATION OF KING EDWARD VII

This photograph shows King Edward VII's Coronation procession crossing Horse Guards Parade. Admiralty Arch, through which later processions have passed, had not then been built.

reminded me so much when I did the same thing to beloved Papa, he did it so well."

Many people will remember the last Coronation, of George VI and Queen Elizabeth, and the perfection of its management by Archbishop Lang, who dominated the ceremony. Within the Abbey it was his day, "in a sense the culminating day of my official life," he wrote. (Not for nothing was he a cousin of Matheson Lang, the actor.) "Once I saw it was going well, I enjoyed every minute," he said. "Thank God that is over!" said his chaplain, as they got into the car to leave. "Lumley, how can you say such a thing!" cried the Archbishop. "I only wish it was all beginning over again."

For the hundreds of thousands of people outside the Abbey, the gold coach with the crowned figures inside brought back something of the element of fairy-tale so wanting in the monochrome of modern life. Well, for us it is all beginning over again, and it is a good thing for our society, and for our kith and kin all over the world, that it should be so: an enacted scene that goes back to the origins of our people, to our earliest memories together, and that expresses the heart of our history.

33

NORMANS

William I
1066–1087

William II
1087–1100

Henry I
1100–1135

Stephen
1135–1154

PLANTAGENETS

HOUSE

Edward I
1272–1307

Edward II
1307–1327

Edward III
1327–1377

Richard II
1377–1399

Henry IV
1399–1413

HOUSE OF TUDOR

Henry VII
1485–1509

Henry VIII
1509–1547

Edward VI
1547–1553

Mary I
1553–1558

Elizabeth I
1558–1603

HOUSE OF HANOVER

George I
1714–1727

George II
1727–1760

George III
1760–1820

George IV
1820–1830

William IV
1830–1837

Victoria
1837–1901

Queen Elizabeth II can trace her royal descent back to William the Conqueror, to Alfred the Great (through the wife of Henry I), and to the Kings of Scotland (through James I). The closing decades of the Plantagenet dynasty, which was descended from Henry I's daughter, were marked by a struggle, known as the Wars of the Roses, between the Yorkist and Lancastrian branches of the family. The final victor was Henry Tudor (Henry VII), a Lancastrian on his mother's side. With the death of Elizabeth I the Crown passed to her distant Stuart

34

PLANTAGENETS

Henry II	Richard I	John	Henry III
1154–1189	1189–1199	1199–1216	1216–1272

HOUSE OF YORK

LANCASTER

Henry V	Henry VI	Edward IV	Edward V	Richard III
1413–1422	1422–1461	1461–1483	1483	1483–1485

HOUSE OF STUART

James I	Charles I	Commonwealth	Charles II	James II	William III and Mary II	Anne
1603–1625	1625–1649	1649–1660	1660–1685	1685–1688	1689–1702 1689–1694	1702–1714

HOUSE OF SAXE-COBURG AND GOTHA   **HOUSE OF WINDSOR**

Edward VII	George V	Edward VIII	George VI	Elizabeth II
1901–1910	1910–1936	1936	1936–1952	acceded 1952

cousin, James VI of Scotland (James I of England), and, after the death of Queen Anne, to the Elector of Hanover (George I), great-grandson of James I. Edward VII, son of Queen Victoria, took the name Saxe-Coburg and Gotha from his father, the Prince Consort. In 1917 George V changed the title to House of Windsor, and Queen Elizabeth II in 1952 reaffirmed this style for herself and her children. (The dates given above are those of reign; a genealogical table which appears on page 46 shows the line of succession from the Tudors to the present day.)

35

KING GEORGE V AT THE DELHI DURBAR, 1911

King George V was the first British monarch with an intimate knowledge of the Commonwealth derived from personal experience. Before he became king he had twice visited Canada, Australia and South Africa, and had been to New Zealand, India and many of the colonies. The idea of a Durbar at Delhi after the Coronation in London was original and his own; his visit proved a great popular success. India has since become independent as a republic, but has remained in the Commonwealth of which she still recognizes the Sovereign as head.

The Queen and the Commonwealth

By SIR THOMAS WHITE, K.B.E., D.F.C., V.D.

WHEN Queen Elizabeth is crowned on 2 June, Australia proposes to adopt the Royal title "Elizabeth the Second by the Grace of God of the United Kingdom, Australia and her other Realms and Territories Queen, Head of the Commonwealth, Defender of the Faith." This epitomizes the whole history of the British monarchy. Australia, having grown quickly from colonial status to an individual State with full and equal rights in the British Commonwealth of Nations, owing no allegiance whatever to the British Parliament of Westminster, not only recognizes the Crown but voluntarily adopts Her Majesty as Queen.

Thus it is that Coronation Day in Australia will be marked and celebrated everywhere as much as in the Mother Country itself. Australians in the deserts around Rum Jungle and the icelands at Macquarie Island in the sub-Antarctic will fly their flags and offer up prayers for Her Majesty's blessing as warmly as those in the national capital. Men, women and children in every State will rejoice together.

And similar celebrations will be held in other Dominions, most of whom propose to adopt similar royal titles. Canada, Australia, New Zealand, South Africa and Ceylon all acknowledge the Queen in their proposed new titles as the head of the Commonwealth. The representatives of all Commonwealth countries concerned have agreed to secure the appropriate constitutional approval for the title changes now envisaged.

How right was the Imperial Conference in 1926 when it declared that "though every Dominion is now and must always remain the sole judge of the nature and extent of its co-operation, no common cause will, in our opinion, be thereby imperilled." The Second World War of 1939–45 demonstrated, if demonstration was needed, the truth of this prophecy. The Commonwealth is not a federation, for there is no central government, defence force and judiciary, and no rigid obligations or commitments. It is not a confederation or an alliance, nor is it comparable with a contractual association such as the United Nations.

A ROYAL WELCOME IN AUSTRALIA

A huge crowd greeted King George VI and Queen Elizabeth (then Duke and Duchess of York) outside Sydney Town Hall during their tour of New Zealand and Australia in 1927.

Like the United Kingdom, the Commonwealth of Nations has no written constitution. There are a number of constitutional conventions, many of which are, in fact, really inhibitions. But all its members are bound together by a common sense of values and ideals and by common interest in the maintenance of peace, and freedom of world security. This broad community of interest arises in part from the fact that each of the Commonwealth nations was at one time the responsibility of the United Kingdom. Sprung thus from a common historical background, they share a common political heritage which in spite of adversities, race and tradition has given rise to a broadly common pattern of institutions, legislation, executive or judiciary.

There are also numerous unofficial links through culture, the professions and sport. The unity through the professions and the pooling of the Commonwealth resources perhaps could not be better illustrated than by the following simple example. The Prime Minister of Ceylon, Mr. D. S. Senanayake, died last year from injuries sustained from a fall from a horse. When he was ill the Ceylon authorities sent for a leading specialist practising in London, who in fact was a New Zealander. When the Shakespeare

Company from Stratford-upon-Avon was touring Australia last summer, Australian artists were performing at Stratford—a further example of the flow of ideas backwards and forwards.

The Queen, at the head of each of the parliaments of the Commonwealth except that of the Republic of India, provides the element of continuity in administration, although her legislative power is a formality. She is in fact a "beacon of unity" for hundreds of millions of people for whom, as the Prime Minister of Australia, Mr. Menzies, said in the New Year, "the flame must burn with a clear and steady light."

Our gracious Queen can trace her ancestry back in an unbroken line for more than eleven hundred years—to an English king called Egbert who ruled England in the ninth century. Possibly we do not realize the significance of this in the feeling we all have of a sense of the continuity of national life. For the constitution of the British Empire, of the British Commonwealth as it is now generally known, has changed considerably over the years; Great Britain has been able to adapt her existing constitutions harmoniously with the changing requirements of time.

In even the last two decades there has been a series of constitutional changes of particular significance to the Commonwealth, the most important being the addition of India and Pakistan in 1947 and of Ceylon in 1948 to the number of independent member states. The issues arising from India's decision to adopt a republican form of constitution, while retaining her membership of the Commonwealth, were met by her acceptance of the Crown as the symbol of the free association of the independent member nations and, as such, the head of the Commonwealth. The basis of the membership of the other Commonwealth countries and their common allegiance to the Crown remained unchanged.

In 1947 Burma decided to become a republic outside the Commonwealth. A year later Eire, too, chose the same

CAPE TOWN CEREMONY
Princess Elizabeth watched from a balcony when King George VI opened Parliament in the Senate Chamber, Cape Town, in February, 1947.

39

path, though by agreement the new Republic of Ireland was not regarded by other Commonwealth countries as a foreign country or her citizens as foreigners. In 1949 Newfoundland chose by plebiscite to enter the confederation of Canada.

Another pointer to the changed ties in the Commonwealth is the fact that Dominions nowadays sometimes choose their Governors-General from their own country. Australia has just had an Australian-born Governor-General in Sir William McKell. Earlier there was Sir Isaac Isaacs. But Australia once more has looked to the Mother Country in Field-Marshal Sir William Slim. In Mr. Vincent Massey Canada has chosen a Governor-General from among her own people.

All this has happened, yet the feeling of continuity remains. Legal ties in the Commonwealth have changed but have been replaced by ties of loyalty and emotion none the less strong, for one reason! It is because, as that distinguished writer on the British constitution, Sir Ernest Barker, so aptly puts it, "Great Britain has the flag of monarchy at her masthead and the ballast of monarchy in her hold. The flag may change its quarter as the ship moves on its long voyage, but it always remains the same flag." And more and more the crew—the people of the Commonwealth—have pulled together in the common cause.

The direct relationship between Crown and Commonwealth has varied vastly even in the last hundred and fifty years. At one time British monarchs turned to Europe, where they were linked by marriage to other monarchs. A monarch seldom made a point of travelling far afield to meet his subjects. Nowadays, however, the emphasis is firmly on the Commonwealth. Sovereigns in the present century have become well known to their people abroad.

King George VI's first-hand knowledge of overseas Commonwealth countries began in 1913 when, at the age of eighteen, he joined the cruiser H.M.S. *Cumberland* for an instructional cruise to the West Indies, Canada and Newfoundland. In later years he met Commonwealth troops at the front in two World Wars, opened the Australian Federal Parliament in 1927 and visited Commonwealth countries in Africa, North America and the Pacific, and continued the tradition created by his father, King George V, of broadcasting to the Commonwealth on Christmas Day.

Queen Elizabeth II continues this same tradition of deep personal concern by the Sovereign in the affairs of the Commonwealth. She accompanied her parents on their tour of South Africa and the Rhodesias in 1947, celebrating her twenty-first birthday at Cape Town. In April, 1949, Princess Elizabeth attended the luncheon at Buckingham Palace for the Commonwealth Prime Ministers and in November visited Malta. In

QUEEN ELIZABETH II WITH HER MINISTERS

Photographed at Buckingham Palace in December, 1952, during a Commonwealth Conference: (*left to right*) Mr. Dudley Senanayake (Ceylon), Sir Godfrey Huggins (Southern Rhodesia), Mr. S. G. Holland (New Zealand), Mr. Winston S. Churchill (United Kingdom), Mr. R. G. Menzies (Australia), Mr. L. S. St. Laurent (Canada), Mr. N. C. Havenga (South Africa), Mr. Khwaja Nazimuddin (Pakistan) and Sir C. Chintaman Deshmukh (India).

October, 1951, the Princess with the Duke of Edinburgh began a coast-to-coast tour of Canada lasting five weeks, and in January, 1952, they left on the first stage of a tour which the King had been unable to carry out because of illness and which was to have taken them to Ceylon, Australia and New Zealand. Later in the same year, as Queen, she welcomed the Prime Ministers of the Commonwealth to a conference in London. Australians now eagerly await the proposed trip of Queen Elizabeth and the Duke of Edinburgh next year, and might even look forward to the day when a Sovereign might have a residence in one or more of the Dominions.

QUEEN ELIZABETH II, BUCKINGHAM PALACE, 1952

The New Elizabethans

By HECTOR BOLITHO

THE year is 1588: we close our eyes and hear the cry of seagulls, and water-fowl, over the river marshes beyond Tilbury. Thirty years have passed since Calais was lost and England is alone: she has no possessions overseas and all the ambition, rivalry and strength of Spain are against her. The arrogant ships of the Armada are ready to cross the Bay of Biscay and ravage the English coast.

We turn from the cry of the seagulls: the salt wind from the Thames Estuary is fresh on our cheeks as we move towards the high bank where Elizabeth's militiamen are encamped—"burying for the present all party distinctions" and ready to resist the violence of Spain. To quicken the hearts of her soldiers for the final ecstasies of battle, the Queen appears among them—a valiant figure, aged fifty-five—on horseback. Riding down between the lines, she pauses, and then she startles the soldiers with the phrases that have since rung through three and a half centuries of Britain's history:

> Let tyrants fear: I have always so behaved myself, that, under God, I have placed my chiefest strength and safeguard in the loyal hearts and good-will of my subjects. And therefore I am come amongst you at this time, not as for my recreation or sport, but being resolved, in the midst and heat of the battle, to live or die amongst you all. . . . I know I have but the body of a weak and feeble woman, but I have the heart of a king, and of a king of England too.

In July, the Armada set out on its great enterprise, but "the feathers of the Spaniards were plucked one by one." "God blew and they were scattered."

Almost two hundred and fifty years pass: the sounds we hear are the clip-clop of horses' hooves in the courtyard of Kensington Palace—before six o'clock in the morning of 20 June, 1837. In those two hundred and fifty years the first British Empire has been made, and lost. England is poor once more and the reputation of the monarchy is low in the land. Queen Victoria does not hear the horses below her bedroom: she is still asleep, and, beyond her window, the night mists still hang about the red-brick façade of the Palace. The young Queen is called by her mother: she leaves her bed and goes into her sitting-room, *alone*, to receive the news of her uncle's death and of her accession. At the end of the day, Queen Victoria writes in her Journal, "I shall do my

43

ELIZABETH I AT TILBURY

Reproduced from an illustration in Thomas Pennant's *Account of London* which was published in 1790.

utmost to fulfil my duty towards my country. I am very young and perhaps in many, though not in all things, inexperienced. But I am sure that very few have more real good-will and more real desire to do what is fit and right than I have."

Our next scene is in New York. Not knowing that a packet-ship is already on its way across the Atlantic, with news of the death of William IV, the English colony is celebrating "Princess" Victoria's eighteenth birthday, with a dinner party. The chief speaker is Captain Marryat, author of *Mr. Midshipman Easy* and many other stirring tales of the sea. He tells the exiles: "I could serve a Queen with even greater zeal and fidelity than I could a King. Indeed, it would appear that women are more calculated to wield the sceptre than men; for, if we refer to our history, we shall find that England never was so great and glorious as under the dynasty of our Queens. . . ."

The gallant captain was not aware that the great and glorious reign of Queen Victoria had already begun.

For our next scene we skip one hundred and ten years, and the setting is Cape Town, on the night of 21 April, 1947. The sky above the city is splendid with fireworks, and Table Mountain is flowing with the silver glow of searchlights. It is still as Drake described it—the "fairest Cape . . . in the whole circumference of the earth." For the first time in history, the heir to the British Throne is to make her coming-of-age declaration in a country of the Commonwealth. Sitting before a microphone, Princess Elizabeth says: "I should like to make that dedication now. It is very simple. I declare before you all that my whole life, whether it be long or short, shall be devoted to your service. . . . God help me to make good my vow. . . ."

On 2 June, within the ancient shadows of Westminster Abbey, Queen Elizabeth II will renew her vow, with even deeper seriousness. We might wonder, in that moment, how far we are justified in the proud belief that the second Elizabethan Age has begun.

PRINCESS VICTORIA HEARS THAT SHE IS QUEEN

The painting reproduced here, which is in the Tate Gallery, London, is among the best-known works of the Victorian painter, Henry Tanworth Wells. He has depicted the scene at Kensington Palace in the early hours of 20 June, 1837, as the Archbishop of Canterbury and the Lord Chamberlain knelt before the young Victoria, still attired in her dressing-gown, and told her of the death of her uncle, King William IV, and of her accession to the throne.

45

GENEALOGICAL TABLE OF THE ROYAL LINE
FROM KING HENRY VII TO QUEEN ELIZABETH II

DATES ARE OF BIRTH AND DEATH

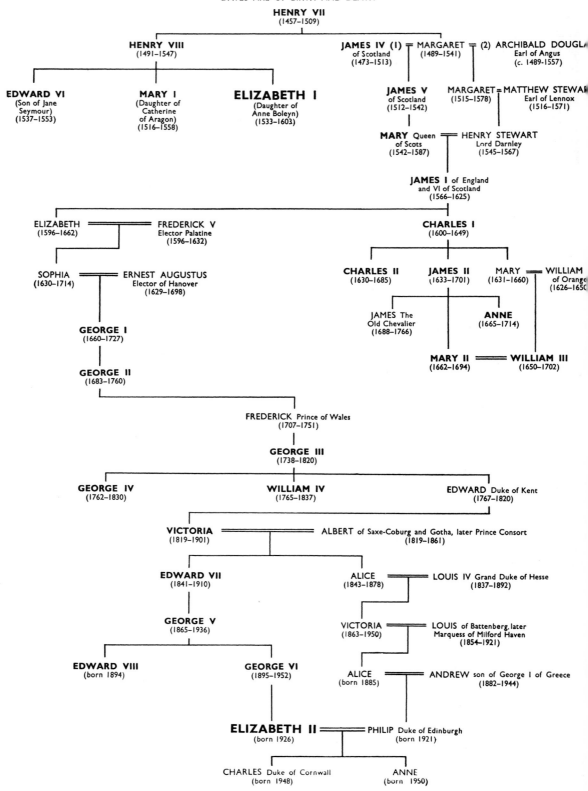

ON THE BALCONY OF BUCKINGHAM PALACE, 8 MAY, 1945

"One of the bells she could hear ringing in a tower of Westminster Abbey . . . had been rung for the defeat of the Armada, in the reign of the first Elizabeth."

It is already true that the name *Elizabeth* quickens the hearts of British adventurers, as it did more than three centuries ago. When Queen Elizabeth II was a child, in her sixth year—in 1931—Sir Douglas Mawson made his great flight in the Antarctic. He saw, "Away to the east-south-east . . . a jumble of large bergs aground," stretching towards an "ice-covered land." When Sir Douglas Mawson flew over the same territory a few days later, the ghost of Sir Francis Drake must have whispered over his shoulder, for he remembered the little Princess in England and he named "this new discovery" *Princess Elizabeth Land.* Twenty-one years later, in September, 1952, twelve British airmen and soldiers were marooned on an ice-cap, 8,000 ft. high, in Greenland. They insulated the fuselage of the crashed aircraft with twelve layers of parachute, but it was still too cold to sleep. When food and drink were dropped to them, they prepared a meal, within the fuselage; and, at the end, the twelve isolated Britons lifted their cups of whisky to the toast of "Her Majesty the Queen."

Between these two episodes of chivalry stretches the story of Queen Elizabeth's life, from the schoolroom to the Throne. It is a story wholly different from that of the first Elizabeth, or of Queen Victoria. We think of the first Elizabeth at the age of twenty-one, sitting on a stone in the rain, at the gate to the Tower, protesting in vain against her imprisonment. And we recall Queen Victoria, growing up through years that were poisoned by the plots of her uncles and the discipline of the schoolroom. In later life she wrote of her "melancholy childhood" and of having been "sad and lonely."

In her own words, the childhood of Queen Elizabeth II was "all sunshine," and this happiness is reflected in almost every episode of her life. But we sense also the growth of will-power behind the happiness, both of which were the natural result of the family life created by her parents. One cannot, in the space of a few thousand words, trace and prove the part played by King George VI and his consort in the development of the monarchy, at a time when its existence was threatened by the example of what was happening in Europe. But we can claim that the King broke one melancholy tradition that goes back to the beginnings of kingship. He created a happy relationship, based on love and trust, with his heir: he proved that it was possible for a sovereign to guard his family happiness and keep the devotion of his successor, in spite of the destroying influences of Court and public life. Queen Elizabeth therefore knows what Queen Victoria never knew: that private happiness and domestic example are not secondary considerations in constitutional monarchy: they are one of the chief reasons why the monarchy survives in British life. A good and happy sovereign provides the apex to the whole structure of the democratic system.

This goodness and happiness have been Queen Elizabeth's blessing, all her life. We see her as a young girl, playing with the children of the foresters at Windsor; we recall her, in her precocious but pretty crown, driving to the Coronation of her father; we think of her, in 1944, launching H.M.S. *Vanguard*—a "brave and winsome figure," watching the great ship move towards the water. Then the gesture, of her hand being raised, rather like her mother, in acknowledgement of the cheering. Then, as the

photographs of her have proved, ever since, the refreshing fact that she was not afraid to smile. Queen Elizabeth has always had the rare talent of being able to share her inward happiness with thousands of people. After the American artist, Douglas Chandor, had painted her portrait, he said: "When she smiles, there is a radiance such as I have seldom seen in any face."

NEARING SOUTH AFRICA
Princess Elizabeth with her father and sister on H.M.S. *Vanguard* as the ship approaches Cape Town.

48

THE QUEEN AND THE DUKE OF EDINBURGH, 1952

AT CLARENCE HOUSE, 1951

(*Above*)
ON THE WAY TO
TROOPING
THE COLOUR, 1952

(*Right*)
PROCLAMATION OF
THE CORONATION,
1952

PRINCE CHARLES, DUKE OF CORNWALL, AGED FOUR

The Princess was eighteen when she launched H.M.S. *Vanguard*: her tasks as heir to the Throne had begun. We turn over the photographs that have given us pleasure during the years since then, and we pause over one of the "famous" balcony—of Buckingham Palace. It was taken on 8 May, 1945. The war was over and, on the balcony, the King and Queen appeared, with Mr. Winston Churchill between them. On their right stood Princess Elizabeth, in A.T.S. uniform. One of the bells she could hear, ringing in a tower of West-

HER DEDICATION

Princess Elizabeth broadcasting to the youth of the Commonwealth from the gardens of Government House, Cape Town, on her twenty-first birthday.

minster Abbey, was more than three hundred and sixty years old; it had been rung for the defeat of the Armada, in the reign of the first Elizabeth.

The next picture shows the Princess on the bridge of H.M.S. *Vanguard*, just before she landed in South Africa, in February, 1947. Then we see a photograph of her, standing beside King George VI, before a house in Natal, and we remark that she is almost as tall as her father. The last of these South African photographs shows her alone, on her twenty-first birthday, before the microphone in Cape Town. She was making the avowal of her courage, in the tradition of her ancestors. Those who like remembering back heard again the gulls crying over Tilbury, and the clip-clop of the horses in the courtyard of Kensington Palace; and they read deep, historical meaning into the twentieth-century promise—"My whole life, whether it be long or short, shall be devoted to your service."

Soon after the Princess returned to England she was betrothed to Prince Philip. If we wondered over her thoughts, and her character, as heir to the Throne and about to be married, we found our answer in a speech that she made about this time. She said: "I do not think you can perform any finer service than to help maintain the Christian doctrine that the relationship of husband and wife is a permanent one, not lightly to be broken because of difficulties or quarrels." Then: "To be cruel to a little child is indeed a dreadful crime." And then: "A good home life is the rock on which a child's future is founded."

In November, 1947, Princess Elizabeth was married, and after her children were born—in November, 1948, and August, 1950—she soon showed that these ideas about marriage, and family life, were to be her own law. The law was not allowed to change when, in January, 1952, the Princess was suddenly called on to assume "a burden from which an archangel might shrink." She flew home from Kenya, to keep both that private law and the promise she had made five years before.

As the day of her Coronation approaches the British will search deeper and deeper into their history, for—more than to any other peoples in the world—the past, the present and the future are one to them.

It is true that, like her namesake, Queen Elizabeth II inherits a crown "entangled with foreign wars." We remember also that when Queen Victoria came to the Throne revolt was beginning in both Upper and Lower Canada. All three Queens began their reigns at a time when almost every voice prophesied war. We search through the story of the Coronation of the first Elizabeth for other parallels, and we come on the touching scene when, after she drove from Cheapside, the Recorder handed the Queen a satin purse, filled with gold. "It required both her hands and all her strength to take it. And the people were delighted to hear her declare: 'Be sure that I will be as good unto you, as ever Queen has been to her people. Persuade yourselves that for the safety and quietness of you all, I will not spare, if need be, to spend my blood.'"

These promises we recognize, in the simpler phrases of our time; in the simpler dedication the second Elizabeth has made. We recognize also the statement that, after Elizabeth I had spoken, her promise so thrilled the people gathered at Cheapside that "it moved a marvellous shout and rejoicing, the *heartiness* of it was so wonderful." Yes, in this we recognize our own emotions, as the ceremonies of June come near.

But, in one circumstance, there is a tremendous difference between these emotions and those stirred at the Coronations of 1559 and 1838. Neither Queen Elizabeth I nor Queen Victoria began their reigns sustained by the affection of good men in every country of the world. And this is young Queen Elizabeth's pleasure. Neither the loyal citizens at Cheapside, nor the crowds watching young Queen Victoria driving through the streets, were the match of us—the new Elizabethans—in our loyalty and delight. In that moment when Queen Elizabeth II is crowned we may be excused if we forget our rivals and our enemies, and think rather of valiant old Captain Marryat, assuring us that "England never was so great and glorious as under the dynasty of our Queens."

THE RADIANT QUEEN

An enchanting moment caught by the camera as Queen Elizabeth drove in the Irish State Coach to carry out the first State Opening of Parliament of her reign, 4 November, 1952.

1926 Mother and Daughter

1927 First Birthday

1928 London Drive

1926 ~ A SOVEREI

1932 At Waldenbury

1933 Birthday Ride

1934 Studio Portrait

1935 Silver Jubilee Wav

1940 Family Group

1941 Windsor Pantomime

1942 At Royal Lodge, Windsor

1943 Sendin

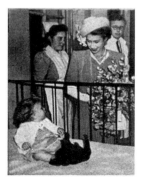

1947 With a Young Patient

1948 First Freewoman of Cardiff

1949 Mother and Son

R

THE MAKING ~ 1952

1929 Three Years Old

1930 Going to a Party

1931 Visit to Olympia

1936 At 145 Piccadilly

1937 After the Coronation

1938 Driving to Church

1939 Prizegiving

...ote by Pigeon Post

1944 At an R.A.F Station

1945 In the A.T.S.

1946 At the Poppy Factory

1950 At the Opera

1951 Garter Ceremony at Windsor

1952 Queen Elizabeth II

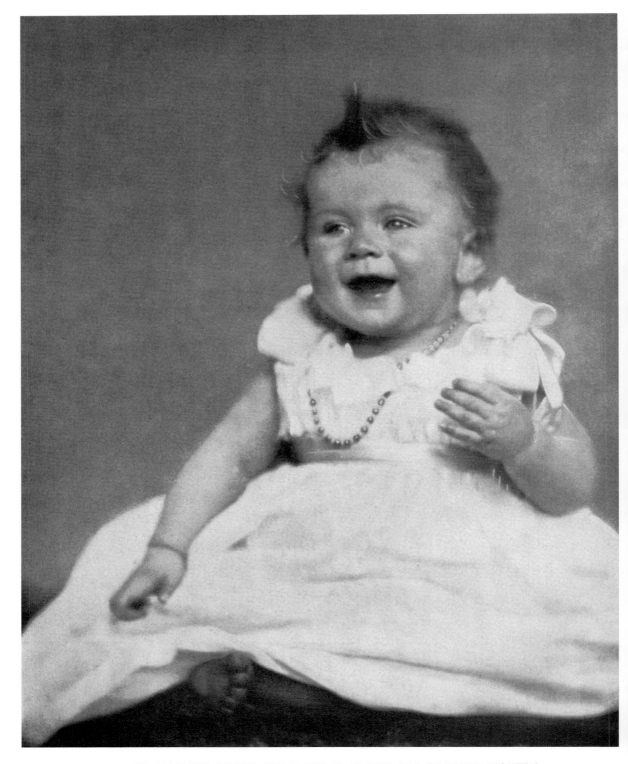

HER MAJESTY QUEEN ELIZABETH II AT THE AGE OF EIGHT MONTHS

The Little Princess

IT WAS not in any palace or royal residence that, on 21 April, 1926, our present Queen was born, but in the London home of her mother's parents, the Earl and Countess of Strathmore and Kinghorne. Some weeks later, on 29 May, she was christened in the private chapel of Buckingham Palace, and given the names Elizabeth Alexandra Mary. In accordance with a tradition dating from the time of the Crusades, the font was filled with water specially brought from the River Jordan.

At her birth the baby Princess ranked third in succession to her grandfather, King George V. But her prospects of accession seemed remote. It was expected that the bachelor Prince of Wales would some day marry and have a family to succeed him; while if her parents later on had a son he would take precedence of any daughters. It was indeed because of this theoretical possibility of a son being born to her father that up to the hour of her accession Princess Elizabeth was only heir-presumptive and never heir-apparent to the Throne.

The British public, however, seemed from the beginning to have an inner conviction that Elizabeth was destined one day to be their Queen, and they took the most affectionate interest in her. Crowds used to gather against the railings shielding the garden of her parents' home at 145, Piccadilly, when as a little toddler of two or three she was at play there; and if she went for a drive round the Serpentine they would mass beside her route, watching for a wave of her baby hand.

Her parents were careful to guard her against being spoilt by this early adulation; and she and her younger sister Margaret passed their childhood years in the happy informality of private home life. An old family servant of the Duchess, Mrs. Clara Knight, who had been her own nursery maid, "Alah," in bygone years, became chief nurse to the little Princesses. Elizabeth was given a Shetland pony when she was four, and started riding. She learned very early to play the piano. Her mother taught her to read, and to speak French. On her sixth birthday the people of Wales presented her with a miniature house, "Y Bwthyn Bach," in which to play. When she was seven Miss Marion Crawford was engaged as her governess, and educated her at home.

But this quiet upbringing was interrupted when, on 10 December, 1936, King Edward VIII abdicated and Elizabeth's father mounted the throne as King George VI. The little ten-year-old Princess became heir-presumptive and went to live in the Palace.

1

5

6

9

7

3

4

8

(1) Stanley Baldwin was Prime Minister. (2) Suzanne Lenglen (*third from left*) was leading woman tennis star. (3) Capt. H. S. Broad won the King's Cup Air Race. (4) Ascot fashions. (5) Labour Party leaders included Arthur Henderson, J. Ramsay MacDonald and J. H. Thomas. (6) Coronach won the Derby. (7) Airships were in fashion. (8) British troops were stationed on the Rhine. (9) Fire destroyed the Shakespeare Memorial Theatre, Stratford-upon-Avon. (10) Open-topped

11

15

12

10

16

13

14

18

17

buses still plied London's streets.
(11) Broadcasting was in its
infancy. (12) Ivor Novello was already a leading actor–
dramatist. (13) The *Mauretania* held the Atlantic Blue
Riband. (14) The Prince of Wales unveiled the
Kitchener Memorial. (15) Rudolph Valentino was
idol of the silent screen. (16) The Duke of York played
in the men's doubles event at the Wimbledon
championships. (17) Cobham flew to South Africa.
(18) Volunteers drove buses in the General Strike.

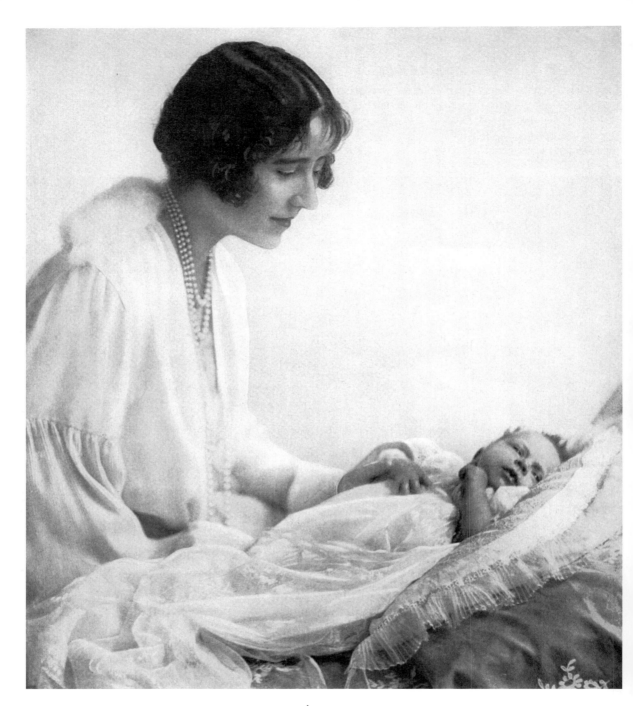

THE KING'S GRANDDAUGHTER

The news of the Princess's birth called forth universal rejoicing in Britain and the Commonwealth, and a warm and friendly interest all over the world. Messages of congratulation poured
in on the King and the Duke and Duchess of York from every quarter. But the deepest
happiness was that of her mother, who tended her baby daughter with loving devotion.

THE TWO-YEAR-OLD

This happy portrait of the Princess was taken in July, 1928. She had now been settled for just over a year with her parents in their new home at 145, Piccadilly, where a top floor was skilfully fitted up as her nursery. On their return in June, 1927, from their Australasian tour, her parents brought back for her three tons of presents from the people of Australia and New Zealand. Many of these were later distributed in her name to children's hospitals.

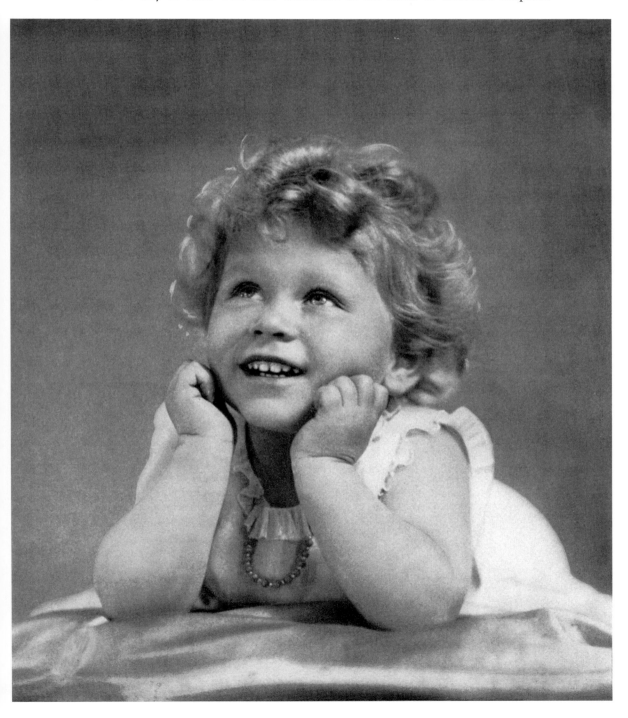

WELCOMED EVERYWHERE

When the baby Princess was taken out in a perambulator into Hyde Park from her Piccadilly home, crowds used to throng about it to such an embarrassing extent that her grandfather, King George V, ordered a landau from the royal mews to be sent round on fine afternoons to drive her around the park. As the picture above shows, this carriage was habitually followed by cheering children, to whom the little Princess would wave her hand. On the left Princess Elizabeth is seen arriving at Glamis in August, 1927, in the arms of her nurse, Mrs. Clara Knight, and being welcomed by the stationmaster, Mr. Buchan. Glamis Castle was the ancestral Scottish home of the Princess's mother, the Duchess of York. It was once held by Macbeth, and is reputed to be the oldest inhabited dwelling in the British Isles. Many grim legends about it are still repeated.

60

MOTHER AND DAUGHTER

This photograph, taken in July, 1929, shows the three-year-old Princess in the arms of her mother. It was the great good fortune of Princess Elizabeth that not alone intelligent guidance but a warm and loving care surrounded her in childhood. Her mother was anxious that her baby daughter should not be left entirely in the care of nurses, however devoted they might be, but should enjoy the happy companionship of her parents as often as possible.

THE SISTERS

Princess Elizabeth and her sister, Princess Margaret, in August, 1932, at their maternal grandparents' home of St. Paul's Waldenbury. Princess Margaret was just two years old. She had been born at Glamis Castle on 21 August, 1930, and bonfires and widespread jubilation had greeted the arrival of the first royal princess born on Scottish soil for three hundred years.

A NURSERY CANTER

Princess Elizabeth takes her sister Margaret for a ride on their rocking-horse. They were from the first the closest of friends, remarkably free from any jealousy or rivalry. For some years legal theorists debated whether, being daughters, they were co-heiresses, but Princess Elizabeth's priority in succession to the Throne was officially announced in 1937.

ROYAL HORSE SHOWS

From her earliest years Princess Elizabeth showed a keen delight in horses. She was given her first pony when she was only four years old and soon became an excellent rider. She is seen above giving an approving pat to a prize-winning pony at the Richmond Horse Show, June, 1934; with her is the late Sir Walter Gilbey, veteran horse-lover. A gala occasion was a visit in the same month to the International Horse Show, Olympia (*left*), with her parents, and her baby sister, Princess Margaret. Behind the Princesses are their nurse, Mrs. Clara Knight, and Wing-Commander Louis Greig. The "Little Duchess," as their mother was affectionately known to many, is hidden behind her husband in this picture, taken on their arrival.

A TOURNAMENT THRILL

The Duke and Duchess of York paid a visit in May, 1935, to the Royal Tournament at Olympia, accompanied by Princess Elizabeth. In the picture above, the Princess is pointing out to a friend an item of particular interest to her in the display of naval gun-drill.

IN A MODEL VILLAGE

Most people, especially children, are fascinated by toy-sized models. On 15 April, 1936, the two Princesses went to Beaconsfield and were shown round the model village of "Bekonscot." They are seen studying the model docks and shipping. Princess Elizabeth seems to display an almost prophetic interest in anything to do with naval affairs.

66

Princess Elizabeth drives back from Crathie Church to Balmoral with her parents and her grandfather, King George V. This picture was taken in August, 1935. It was their last summer together, for in the following January the King died. Though somewhat of a disciplinarian, he was always extremely fond of his little granddaughter, and much more indulgent to her than he had been to his own children. When he was slowly convalescing at Bognor Regis from a very serious illness, at the end of 1928, he specially asked for little Princess Elizabeth to be brought there to keep him company, and her prattle and play and warm affection were his best medicine. Her cheerful companionship did a great deal toward speeding his recovery.

A KING DEPARTS

The year 1936 brought drama and tragedy to the Royal Family. In January King George V died, and the Prince of Wales ascended the throne as King Edward VIII. Never had there been a prince more personally popular, not only in the Empire and Commonwealth, but in foreign countries. Yet he found the burden of kingship too heavy, and before the year was out he decided for personal reasons to renounce all title to the throne for himself and his descendants. On 10 December he abdicated, and his brother, the Duke of York, reluctantly consented to replace him. This development made the Princess Elizabeth the immediate heir to the throne. The upper picture on the left shows King Edward making his first broadcast after his accession. Below are seen the crowds that lingered outside Buckingham Palace when the crisis in his monarchy had arisen; and the arrival of the Duke of York at his home in 145, Piccadilly, when he hastened back to urge his brother not to abdicate. The Princess Elizabeth and her sister are shown above, playing untroubled on 19 December, 1936, in their garden, heedless of the portentous events that were to bring about so great a change in their destiny.

PRINCESS ELIZABETH AT TROOPING THE COLOUR, 12 JUNE, 1947

70

The King's Heir

THE accession of her father as King George VI brought a dramatic change in the position of the ten-year-old Princess Elizabeth. From being only a potential heir to the throne she became at a stroke the immediate heir, next in succession. One of the reasons which made the Duke of York reluctant to accept the Crown was the realization that he was thereby fore-ordaining his little daughter to the heavy burdens of monarchy.

After Christmas, 1936, the new King and his family moved into Buckingham Palace. Inevitably the Princess had now to appear more frequently with her parents at public functions; but these were allowed to interfere as little as possible with her quiet education and training at home. Then came the war, its flames slowly spreading till the whole world was in conflagration. Princess Elizabeth and her sister spent the war years mostly at Windsor Castle. When she was thirteen her education by Miss Crawford was reinforced with the help of the Provost of Eton, who gave her special training in constitutional history—a particularly important study for a future monarch. At the age of sixteen she formally signed on for National Service at the Windsor Labour Exchange; but the Government considered that her best war work would be to continue her education for the tasks lying ahead of her.

The Princess was eighteen years old in April, 1944, and she carried out her first public engagement independently of her parents on 23 May, at the annual meeting of Queen Elizabeth's Hospital for Children. In July she was appointed a Counsellor of State during the King's visit to the Italian front, and in November she christened the battleship *Vanguard* at its launching. In the following spring she was commissioned in the A.T.S., and learned driving and maintenance of mechanical transport.

When hostilities ended, London plunged into a joyful post-war whirl of gaiety, dancing and social functions, at which people noticed that Princess Elizabeth was often to be seen in the company of a strikingly handsome young naval officer, Prince Philip of Greece, who was her third cousin on his mother's side. Progress of their romance was interrupted during the early part of 1947, when the King and Queen took their two daughters with them on an official visit to South Africa. But within two months of their return, on 9 July, 1947, the King announced his consent to their betrothal. On 20 November they were married in Westminster Abbey.

A VISIT TO THE NATIONAL MARITIME MUSEUM, GREENWICH

King George VI, accompanied by Queen Elizabeth, Queen Mary and Princess Elizabeth, went to Greenwich on 27 April, 1937, for the ceremonial opening of the National Maritime Museum. The Museum houses a collection of relics and records of naval history and maritime art of Great Britain from the earliest times. They voyaged from Westminster Pier in an Admiralty barge—a method of travel which was habitually adopted in Tudor and Stuart times, when the royal barge was often to be seen up and down London's busy river.

AT A CORONATION CONCERT

The Coronation of King George VI took place on 12 May, 1937, in a scene of splendid pageantry and an atmosphere of national rejoicing. Coronation festivities began some time before the actual ceremony, and on 6 April a concert for children was held at the Central Hall, Westminster, to which the Queen took her two daughters. Completely enthralled by the music, Princess Elizabeth is sitting on the right-hand side of her mother.

72

CORONATION NAVAL REVIEW

Princess Elizabeth accompanies her royal parents aboard H.M.S. *Victoria and Albert* to witness the 1937 Review of the Fleet at Portsmouth. Her new status as next heir to the throne made it desirable for her to be present more frequently at such national ceremonies, and to grow accustomed to their routine and the part the monarch should play in them. But most of her time was still passed, as before, in strict attention to study during the mornings, and to riding, walking, games and other useful recreations in the afternoons. She liked music and drawing.

A DRIVE WITH HER GRANDMOTHER

The twelve-year-old Princess drives with Queen Mary to watch the Trooping the Colour ceremony in 1938. There has always been a deep bond of affection and understanding between the two, and Princess Elizabeth could have had no wiser mentor to guide her on her royal pathway.

PLANTING A TREE

The Princesses were at Glamis Castle, their mother's early home, in the autumn of 1937, and Princess Elizabeth planted a yew tree in the grounds. A yew tree is long-lasting and may live a thousand years.

A TRIP IN THE ROYAL YACHT

This picture, taken on 30 July, 1938, shows the King and Queen and the two Princesses being greeted at Cowes when the King's yacht put in for a surprise visit. The royal party landed from the yacht by motor-launch, and only spent a few minutes ashore before resuming their sail. King George VI had originally been trained for the Navy, and never lost his love of the sea. As a midshipman he was distinguished for his skill in the handling of small craft.

"LUCKY DIP" FOR THE PRINCESS

At a fancy-dress party for children, given by the Viscountess Astor in St. James's Square on 7 March, 1939, Princess Elizabeth is seen trying the "lucky dip." Like most girls, the Princess delighted in dressing up and wearing fancy costumes. During the war years she greatly enjoyed the succession of Christmas plays and pantomimes at Windsor Castle, in which she performed, usually taking the part of "Principal Boy." In the last of these wartime productions, however, she appeared as a beauty of the Edwardian era.

A VISIT TO NUMBER 145

An exhibition of royal treasures was organized in 1939 at His Majesty's old home, 145, Piccadilly. Princess Elizabeth and her sister paid a visit to it and inspected their old nursery, where they had played as children, before they went to live in a royal palace.

A BIRTHDAY RIDE IN WINDSOR PARK

Princess Elizabeth was always at home in the saddle. Before she was six years old she took every opportunity that offered to ride in Windsor Great Park. By preference she rides astride, as in this picture, which shows her on her thirteenth birthday riding at Windsor with her father. On ceremonial occasions, however, she adopts the traditional side-saddle.

WARTIME AT WINDSOR

Contrary to a tale industriously broadcast for some time by Dr. Goebbels, the Nazi propagandist, Princess Elizabeth and her sister were never evacuated to Canada during the war. Its outbreak found them up in Scotland, at Balmoral Castle, where they stayed on for some months; but by Christmas, 1939, they had come south to Windsor, and here they remained till the war was drawing to an end. Their parents joined them whenever they could leave London. The Princesses' life here was quiet, but by no means idle. Regular hours were devoted to study. Lessons began at 9.30 each morning. In the afternoons there would be drawing, sketching or serious reading, and written preparation occupied part of the evenings. But in fine weather much of the afternoon work would be done in the open air. The Princesses are seen (*top, left*) on a sunny afternoon in September, 1941, reading in Windsor Park. Later on they took one of their Corgis for a short drive in the park (*centre, left*). The other two pictures were taken in May, 1944. The sisters are making friends with a pair of ponies (*top, right*), while the Queen and Princess Elizabeth are pictured (*bottom, left*) in Queen Alexandra's chaise.

78

IN THE GIRL GUIDES

When Princess Elizabeth reached the age of sixteen, in April, 1942, she conformed to the regulations laid down in the National Service Act, and went to the Windsor office of the Ministry of Labour (*right*) to register for National Service. She completed the customary buff form, naming as her Youth Organization the Girl Guides. In the crew of Sea Rangers to which she belonged Princess Elizabeth had already earned several badges for proficiency and had reached the rank of bosun. In the picture below she is seen taking the tiller in the course of Sea Ranger boating exercises. The Girl Guide organization gave the Princess a welcome means of allying herself with other girls of her own age, and thus making friendly contact with those over whom she would one day be called on to reign. In fact, only ten short years were to pass before Princess Elizabeth assumed the responsibilities of the Throne.

SUBALTERN IN THE A.T.S.

In April, 1944, Princess Elizabeth reached her eighteenth birthday, and officially came "of age" as royal heiress. She could now undertake the full tasks of monarchy if called on. (Queen Victoria was just eighteen when she ascended the throne.) In July King George VI appointed the Princess a Counsellor of State during his absence in Italy. Otherwise her coming of age brought little immediate change in her activities. It was officially announced that she would not join one of the Women's Services or be sent to work in a munition factory. But she herself was most unwilling to accept this decision, and before a year had passed she persuaded the King to gazette her as a second subaltern in the Auxiliary Territorial Service. She was posted to the No. 1 Mechanical Transport Training Centre to take a full course in driving and car maintenance and repair. The Princess proved an apt pupil, and like her father she showed a keen interest in mechanical and engineering processes. She quickly became an excellent driver, and mastered the chief tasks of a motor mechanic, such as adjusting carburettors, grinding-in valves, decarbonizing engines and carrying out running repairs. She is shown on the left beside her instruction car. In the picture above she is changing a car's plugs.

THE HOUR OF TRIUMPH

When, after nearly six years of unparalleled suffering, terror and desperate resistance, Britain won through to victory in the Second World War, there was no limit to the nation's relief and exultation. Germany surrendered on 8 May, 1945 (VE-day), and dense multitudes thronged before Buckingham Palace, loyally cheering the King. Japan's surrender followed on 15 August, and the picture above shows the Royal Family on the Palace balcony on VJ-day. The lower picture shows a section of the happy crowd which assembled then.

REMEMBRANCE DAY, 11 NOVEMBER, 1945

Two World Wars within a single generation have made the Cenotaph in Whitehall a sad though proud symbol of sacrifice from which few families in the kingdom have remained exempt; and the annual ceremony there strikes a deeper chord than that of pageantry. Princess Elizabeth is here seen in the uniform of a Junior Commander of the A.T.S., laying her wreath in tribute to the fallen, on the first Armistice Day after the end of the Second World War.

VICTORY PARADE,
8 JUNE, 1946

While popular celebrations followed instantly on the close of hostilities, the ceremonial Victory Parade waited until the next summer, when it was held in London with majestic pageantry. Churchill tanks are shown passing the saluting base in the Mall, where the King took the salute. The upper picture shows Queen Mary, Princess Elizabeth, King George VI and Queen Elizabeth standing on the royal dais. Below, the King and Queen receive Mr. Winston Churchill and Mr. Attlee at the base.

FESTIVITIES OF PEACE

The fighting over, people everywhere turned to laughter and gaiety, to dancing and social enjoyment—although the continuing food shortage restricted their ability to feast. Princess Elizabeth entered gaily into this reviving social life, and was a familiar figure at various Society functions. On the right she is photographed dining at the "Bagatelle," in December, 1945. Beside her is the Honourable Margaret Elphinstone.

AT THE COMMANDO BALL

The young men who during the war had been hourly facing death, and engaging in exploits that fiction would not dare to rival, flung themselves into their well-earned enjoyment of post-war life with eager zest. London Society resumed by degrees its round of entertainments, somewhat hampered by the fact that nearly everyone now had work on hand. In June, 1946, the Commandos gave a ball at which Princess Elizabeth was a very welcome guest. She is here seen at supper with members of her party.

A MOUNTBATTEN WEDDING

On many social occasions Princess Elizabeth was frequently accompanied by a young naval lieutenant, Prince Philip of Greece, a nephew of Lord Louis Mountbatten. In 1946 the Royal Family attended the wedding of Lord Louis's daughter, Patricia, at Romsey Abbey; the two Princesses were bridesmaids and Prince Philip escorted them.

86

WEDDING GUESTS, MAY, 1946

Princess Elizabeth was bridesmaid to her Lady-in-Waiting, the Honourable Mrs. Vicary Gibbs, on the occasion of her marriage to Captain the Honourable Andrew Elphinstone, nephew of the Queen. Prince Philip is pictured with her at the reception at the Savoy.

THE PRINCESS AT HOME

These pictures were taken at Buckingham Palace on 19 July, 1946. Although the number of official engagements which Princess Elizabeth had to fulfil increased steadily following her emergence into public affairs, she was able to enjoy brief periods of relaxation in the privacy of her own sitting-room. The Royal Family are eager philatelists, and the Princess is seen (*left*) examining additions to her stamp-album. Time for serious reading is limited, but, as the picture below shows, when she has the opportunity the Princess likes to settle down comfortably to concentrate on a book.

GENERAL EISENHOWER AT BALMORAL

General Eisenhower, supreme commander of the allied assault on North-west Europe in 1944, visited the King at Balmoral Castle (*above*) in October, 1946; his wife and his son accompanied him. Six years later the General retired from the Army in order to accept nomination for the Presidency of the United States. He was elected in November, 1952.

King George VI, accompanied by Queen Elizabeth and the two Princesses, sailed on 1 February, 1947, in the new battleship, H.M.S. *Vanguard*, to pay a State visit to South Africa. Very rough weather was encountered in the Bay of Biscay and the *Vanguard* suffered minor damage. This was not serious, however, and soon the ship sailed into calm waters and a warmer climate. The royal party could then enjoy the sports and pastimes of ocean travel. On the left Princess Elizabeth is seen practising rifle shooting, and below is a picture of the royal travellers sunning themselves on *Vanguard's* quarter-deck. On the right King

VOYAGE TO SOUTH AFRICA

George and the two Princesses are inspecting the contents of a hamper of fresh tropical fruit, a present from the people of Sierra Leone, which H.M.S. *Nigeria* brought when she came for escort duties off Freetown. The *Vanguard* reached the equator on 10 February, and the lower picture is of a scene during the traditional ceremonies carried out on board a ship when she crosses the line. King Neptune presides, and it is customary for newcomers haled before him to be ducked in a tank. Princess Elizabeth and her sister were, however, excused the ducking, and were allowed to take their medicine in the more palatable form of a pill.

SHIP'S KITTENS ENJOY ROYAL FAVOUR

Minnie, ship's cat in H.M.S. *Vanguard*, had a family on the voyage, and Princess Elizabeth is here seen fondling a pair of the kittens under their mother's approving eye. From her earliest years the Princess was always very fond of animals and loved playing with them. At home at Windsor the household dogs were constantly to be found romping in her company.

OPENING A NEW DOCK

The royal party landed at Cape Town on 17 February, to receive a tumultuous welcome from great crowds of the many races and colours inhabiting South Africa. On 21 February the King opened the Union Parliament and then took the Queen and Princesses on a tour of the Cape Province. At East London, on 3 March, Princess Elizabeth was called upon to perform the ceremony of opening a new graving dock in the harbour, named in her honour the "Princess Elizabeth Dock." She is seen (right) declaring the dock open, and below she stands beside the newly-inscribed name-stone.

IN NATAL NATIONAL PARK

The royal visitors travelled from the Cape Province through the Orange Free State and visited Basutoland. They returned on 13 March and were received at Harrismith by Field-Marshal Smuts; he travelled with them to Ladysmith, and they then spent a few days resting at a hostel in the Natal National Park, a wild-life reserve. The picture (*top, left*) shows Princess Elizabeth with her father and sister in the grounds of this hostel; she is seen (*top, right*) on her South African pony, enjoying a ride along the sands at Bonza Bay, East London. The lower picture, also taken in Natal National Park, is a charmingly happy one of the Princess sitting reading in the sunlight. Behind her tower the heights of the Drakensberg Mountains. While the royal party was resting in the National Park the news came through that Prince Philip of Greece had renounced his foreign titles and had been granted British citizenship. He would in future be known as Lieutenant Philip Mountbatten, R.N.

94

DIAMONDS WORTH MILLIONS

The Royal Family visited the diamond mines of Kimberley on 18 April, on their way back from Southern Rhodesia. An assortment of stones worth £3,000,000 was displayed to them by the Chairman of the De Beers Consolidated Mines, Ltd., and Princess Elizabeth is seen examining one of them. They travelled on to Cape Town, where on 21 April Princess Elizabeth celebrated her twenty-first birthday. The day was made a public holiday throughout the Dominion. The Princess reviewed a parade of the South African Army, and later broadcast a message to the people of the Commonwealth, dedicating her future life to their service. In the evening there were firework displays, and a State Ball was given at Government House.

WEDDING PORTRAIT, BUCKINGHAM PALACE, 20 NOVEMBER, 1947

Duchess of Edinburgh

THERE was delighted satisfaction at the news of Princess Elizabeth's engagement. People not only welcomed the romance of a love match; they were happy, too, that their future Queen had found a mate so capable, virile and attractive. The wedding took place in Westminster Abbey on 20 November, 1947, in a setting of magnificent pageantry. Previously the King had restored Philip's royal status as His Royal Highness and made him Duke of Edinburgh, Earl of Merioneth and Baron Greenwich, and a Knight of the Garter.

Honeymoon over, they had many public engagements to fulfil. In May, 1948, they paid a State visit to Paris, as guests of the French Government. On 14 November Princess Elizabeth gave birth to a son, who was named Charles Philip Arthur George. People generally, and the Scots in particular, were delighted at having once again a Prince Charles. Soon after the Prince's birth King George fell ill, and his proposed tour of Australia and New Zealand had to be postponed. During the early part of 1949 the Duke of Edinburgh stayed in Britain and accompanied Princess Elizabeth to a number of public functions. In October he rejoined the Navy in the Mediterranean, and Princess Elizabeth went out twice to Malta to visit him—in November, and in the following spring. On 15 August, 1950, their second child, Princess Anne, was born.

The Duke, who was at home for this happy event, returned soon afterwards to the Mediterranean in command of H.M.S. *Magpie*, and in the winter the Princess joined him for a cruise, in which they visited Athens. The Duke ended his active service with the Navy in July, 1951, and came home. In the autumn they were about to sail on an official visit to Canada when King George's illness, and the serious operation he had to undergo in September, postponed their departure. As soon as His Majesty was safely over the operation they flew the Atlantic, arriving in Quebec only a week behind the date originally planned, and made a coast-to-coast tour of the Dominion amid scenes of the greatest enthusiasm. They also paid a three-day visit to Washington as guests of President Truman.

The Royal Family were together at Sandringham for Christmas. At the end of January, 1952, Princess Elizabeth and her husband left for a State visit to East Africa, Ceylon and Australasia. They were still in Kenya when the news reached them on 6 February that King George VI had passed away.

THE ROYAL LOVERS

There was never any doubt in people's minds that Princess Elizabeth's heart and hand had gone together in her acceptance of Philip Mountbatten as her future husband. The happy picture above is the first taken of the two after the King had formally announced their betrothal. The Princess is proudly wearing her engagement ring for the first time.

ROYAL GARDEN PARTY

On the day of the announcement of their engagement, 10 July, 1947, Princess Elizabeth and her fiancé attended a Royal Garden Party at Buckingham Palace; many guests surrounded them to offer their congratulations and warm good wishes.

EDINBURGH VISIT

In July the Royal Family took up residence at Holyroodhouse, and on the 16th Princess Elizabeth received the Freedom of Edinburgh at Usher Hall. On the same day, accompanied by Lieutenant Mountbatten, she visited the Argyll and Sutherland Highlanders Club, where Brigadier H. J. D. Clark (*right*) presented the Princess with a regimental brooch in diamonds.

99

WEDDING OF PRINCESS ELIZABETH: 20 NOVEMBER, 1947

The marriage of Princess Elizabeth, heir to the British throne, and Prince Philip, Duke of Edinburgh, was celebrated in Westminster Abbey in stately and magnificent fashion. The ceremony was conducted by the Archbishop of Canterbury, in the presence of kings and queens from other lands, of Britain's most distinguished leaders, and of outstanding figures from the Commonwealth, including Field-Marshal Smuts, Premier of South Africa, and Mr. Mackenzie King, Premier of Canada. On the eve of the wedding the bridegroom, Lieutenant Philip Mountbatten, formerly Prince Philip of Greece, had his royal rank restored by the King and was created Duke of Edinburgh. He is seen on the extreme left arriving at the Abbey. The other two pictures on the left show Queen Elizabeth and Princess Margaret alighting at the West door, and Princess Elizabeth being escorted to the Abbey by the King. Above is the scene at the altar steps during the ceremony, where the familiar vows were made.

101

From early dawn on the wedding-day enormous crowds were packed beside the route, the whole way between Buckingham Palace and Westminster Abbey, and there were remarkable demonstrations of national rejoicing at the happy culmination of Princess Elizabeth's romance. The event was made by the authorities the occasion for a gay return from wartime austerity to the full colour and pageantry of State ceremonial. The Household Cavalry wore again their tunics of scarlet or blue, their glittering breastplates and plumed helmets. The Abbey sacrarium was adorned with its richest treasures of gold plate. But the marriage ceremony followed the same simple lines as those of a wedding in any village church. The same familiar vows were exchanged; and when it was over, the newly married couple left the Abbey in a bridal coach for the wedding reception at Buckingham Palace. Crowds still waited, lining the streets, to watch as Princess Elizabeth and the Duke drove away in the afternoon to Waterloo, on their way to spend the first part of their honeymoon at Broadlands, Earl Mountbatten's home near Romsey in Hampshire. They drove in an open carriage, seated high, and as they waved their acknowledgements of the onlookers' plaudits they presented a memorable picture of utterly radiant happiness. At Broadlands, however, they found it difficult to escape from well-meaning sightseers, and for the second part of their honeymoon they went to Birkhall, near Balmoral. Many thousand of wedding presents poured in on them, and a display of these was held at St. James's Palace. Admission fees to this display provided a large sum for distribution to a number of charities in which Princess Elizabeth was specially interested—in some cases as their Patron.

ROYAL HONEYMOON

After the pageantry and the ceremonial, the formal photographs and the reception, the royal wedding-day ended with the same final farewell as that given to every newly-wed couple leaving for their honeymoon. The Princess and her husband were pelted with rose-petals at Buckingham Palace as they took their seats in an open carriage to drive to the station. Rose-petals are a kindlier shower than the rice which used in their grandparents' time to be flung at bride and groom in painful good-will.

WEDDING PICTURES

In the peace and quietude of Broadlands the Princess and the Duke were able to enjoy a few precious weeks of leisure, and to readjust themselves for the new life they would henceforth face in partnership. They are seen here examining a batch of photographs that had been taken on their wedding-day. Like her father, Princess Elizabeth had always found photography a fascinating subject, and she had taken many informal snapshots for her personal picture album.

PLANNING FOR THEIR FUTURE

Deep in discussion, Princess Elizabeth and Prince Philip stroll in the autumn sunshine. King George VI had granted them Clarence House as a residence, but as it needed extensive overhaul and refitting they set up a temporary home, when their honeymoon was over, at Windlesham Moor, near Sunningdale. Here they were within easy reach of London, but in the quiet charm of the Surrey countryside. They eventually moved to Clarence House in early 1949.

A VISIT TO FRANCE

At the invitation of President Auriol, Princess Elizabeth and Prince Philip paid a State visit to Paris at Whitsuntide, 1948. They were greeted with the utmost warmth by great crowds when they arrived on 14 May, and the Princess opened an exhibition depicting British life in Paris. On following days they visited Versailles, and attended receptions at the British and Canadian Embassies; on Whit Sunday afternoon they watched racing at Longchamp. The Princess is here shown with President Auriol, who presented her with the Grand Cross of the Legion of Honour. Below, the royal visitors are laying a wreath on the tomb of the Unknown Soldier. At the right is seen General Giraud.

A GALA NIGHT AT THE OPERA

After visiting Fontainebleau on Whit Monday, 17 May, the Prince and Princess attended a gala evening of the ballet at the Paris Opera House. Although Princess Elizabeth was making her first visit to France, she had been so well tutored by her mother that she could speak faultless French. Prince Philip had passed his early boyhood in Paris and naturally was quite at his ease there. Enthusiastic crowds waited to catch a glimpse of the royal guests.

A PARISIAN WELCOME

The upper picture shows a cheering throng on the balcony of a house beside the route followed by Princess Elizabeth and Prince Philip when they attended a reception given by the Paris Municipal Council. Brilliant draperies were hung out to decorate the streets as the royal visitors passed. On the right the Prince and Princess are seen in the Presidential Grandstand at the Longchamp racecourse, acknowledging the acclamations of the crowd. Beside them stands Mme Auriol, the wife of the French President. This visit of the royal couple did a great deal to deepen the friendship which had always existed between France and Britain.

107

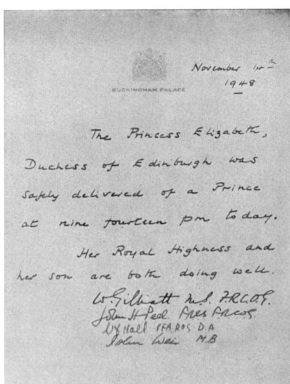

November 14th
1948

The Princess Elizabeth, Duchess of Edinburgh was safely delivered of a Prince at nine fourteen pm to-day.

Her Royal Highness and her son are both doing well.

W. Gilliatt M.S. F.R.C.O.G.
John H Peel. Pres F.R.C.O.S.
Vy Hall FFA.ROS D.A
John Weir M.B

BIRTH OF PRINCE CHARLES

After returning from Paris, Princess Elizabeth began to restrict her public engagements. She received the degree of Doctor of Civil Law at Oxford on 25 May, and the Freedom of the City of Cardiff two days later, but during the late summer and autumn she remained in retirement. On 14 November, 1948, she gave birth to a son; expectant crowds gathered outside Buckingham Palace, and thronged to read the good news of the doctors' bulletin. A section of the crowd, shown in the lower picture, appealed for a speech by the Duke of Edinburgh. Shortly before the birth of Prince Charles an announcement had been made by the King that any children born to Prince Philip and Princess Elizabeth should bear the style of His or Her Royal Highness. Normally in England the children of the monarch's daughters, unlike those of his sons, do not enjoy royal rank; but in this case it was clear that, as Princess Elizabeth was the immediate heir to the throne, her children would be next in royal succession after her before any other prince or princess.

PRINCESS ELIZABETH AND HER SON

This picture was taken on 15 December, 1948, the day on which the baby Prince was christened. The ceremony was conducted by the Archbishop of Canterbury in Buckingham Palace, and the boy was named Charles Philip Arthur George. He had eight godparents: King George VI, King Haakon of Norway, Queen Mary, Princess Margaret, Prince George of Greece, the Dowager Lady Milford Haven, the Honourable David Bowes-Lyon and Lady Brabourne.

ROYAL GREETING FOR BALLERINA

Christmas, 1948, was spent by the Royal Family at Buckingham Palace and in January they went down to spend some weeks at Sandringham. On 1 March, 1949, Princess Elizabeth travelled with Prince Philip to Edinburgh, where he was made a Freeman of the City and she received an honorary degree at the University. A Royal Command charity concert was held in the Usher Hall, at which the Princess is seen (*above*) greeting the ballerina, Moira Shearer.

THE PRINCESS AT NOTTINGHAM

In November, 1948, King George VI fell ill with defective blood circulation in his legs. Prince Philip had to postpone his return to the Navy, and he and Princess Elizabeth represented the King in the months that followed at a number of public functions. On 28 June, 1949, they visited Nottingham during a tour of the North Midlands; the Princess is seen (*right*) leaning across the barrier for a talk with the Deputy Lord Mayor, Councillor J. E. Mitchell, during a display of folk-dancing in Forest Park. She is herself very fond of dancing.

HOW BOATS ARE BUILT

Princess Elizabeth and Prince Philip paid a visit, on 6 July, 1949, to the Royal Agricultural Show at Shrewsbury. The Princess is here seen touring the Rural Industries section of the Show, and questioning a craftsman about the method of construction of a fisherman's boat. Prince Philip stands some distance away. He is expert in the handling and repair of small craft, and as a schoolboy used to sail them off the Scottish coast. Once he made a trip across to Norway in a fishing-smack.

AMONG THE YORKSHIRE MILLS

From 26 to 28 July the Prince and Princess carried out a three-day tour of the West Riding of Yorkshire, visiting Halifax, Huddersfield, Pudsey, Leeds, Wakefield, Harrogate and York. The Prince was free to resume his naval duties shortly afterwards. At the "Halifax for Britain" Exhibition the Princess pauses by the stand of the Yorkshire Master Cotton Spinners' and Doublers' Association to inspect one of the fabrics manufactured by a member firm of the Association for the export trade.

111

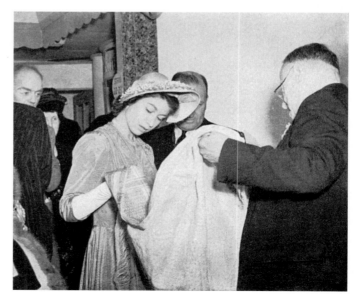

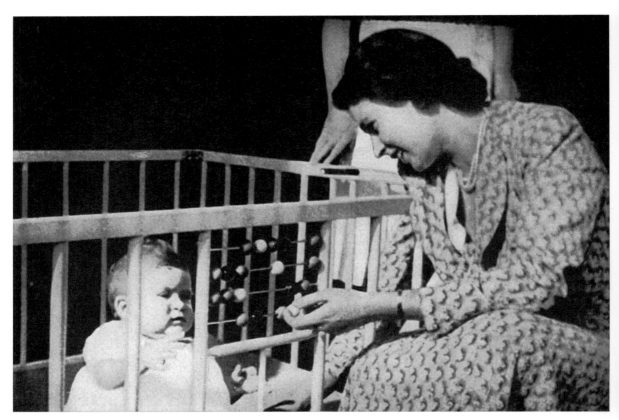

PROUD PARENTS

On 4 July, 1949, Princess Elizabeth and the Duke of Edinburgh were able to take up residence at Clarence House, their London home beside St. James's Palace, which had at last been got ready for them. Much had to be done before it was fit for occupation, and they were both insistent on the alterations conforming to their ideas. These two pictures were among the last taken at their home at Windlesham Moor before they vacated it for Clarence House. Princess Elizabeth (*above*) watches Prince Charles in his playpen; The Duke of Edinburgh (*left*) lifts him carefully out of his perambulator in the garden.

112

PRINCE CHARLES PLAYS "I SPY"

This merry picture catches Princess Elizabeth and her son in the act of peeping round a pillar in the grounds of Buckingham Palace to wave a greeting to another member of the family. It was taken in 1950, when the little Prince was in his second year. The good companionship existing between mother and child, particularly important in babyhood, is here very apparent.

THE PRINCESS VISITS HER HUSBAND IN MALTA

Prince Philip was eager to get back to his naval career, and in October, 1949, he returned to the Mediterranean as first lieutenant in H.M.S. *Chequers*. But Princess Elizabeth had no mind to be separated for a long stretch of time from her husband, and in November she flew out to join him for a short holiday in Malta. This was the first visit she had made to this famous island; they stayed in the small but lovely Villa Guardamangia, enjoying again for a few days the happiness of married life, and are seen here walking in the Villa garden. After Christmas the Prince had to sail away in H.M.S. *Chequers* to the Red Sea, and the Princess flew home. But in the spring of 1950 she came back again to spend some days with him in Malta.

114

BIRTH OF PRINCESS ANNE

On 15 August, 1950, a second child was born to Princess Elizabeth. The baby girl was christened at Buckingham Palace on 21 October, and given the names Anne Elizabeth Alice Louise. The picture shows (*back row*) Lord Louis Mountbatten, Princess Margarita (sister of the Duke of Edinburgh) and the Honourable Andrew Elphinstone. Seated next to Princess Elizabeth are Princess Alice of Athlone and the Queen, with Prince Charles in the foreground.

OPENING THE FESTIVAL OF BRITAIN

The 1951 Festival of Britain, commemorating the centenary of the Great Exhibition of 1851, was declared open by King George VI from the steps of St. Paul's Cathedral on 3 May. In the evening an inaugural concert of British music was held in the Royal Festival Hall on South Bank, and the King also unveiled a commemorative tablet. This picture shows members of the royal party arriving at the Hall for the concert. With Princess Elizabeth and the Duke of Edinburgh are the Princess Royal, Princess Margaret and the Duchess of Gloucester.

THE PRINCESS TRAVELS ABROAD

In the autumn of 1950, after the birth of Princess Anne, the Duke of Edinburgh returned to the Mediterranean in command of his own ship, the frigate H.M.S. *Magpie*. Princess Elizabeth again went out to join him, and during a short cruise they visited Athens, where they were welcomed by the King and Queen of Greece. In April, 1951, she left England again to fly with Prince Philip on a visit to Rome. On 13 April the Prince and Princess were granted a private audience with the Pope, Pius XII, and are seen here in the Vatican. For nearly half an hour they conversed, in English, with the Pope, and afterwards toured the Vatican museums and the Sistine chapel. Princess Elizabeth flew home, returning on 24 April.

GUARDSMEN ON PARADE

On her return from her travels abroad Princess Elizabeth resumed her home duties at Clarence House, the care of her children, and an almost incessant round of attendances at public functions, parades, exhibitions, annual meetings and so on. She took part in the ceremonial opening of the Festival of Britain on 3 May, and in the reception and entertainment of the King and Queen of Denmark when they arrived in England on 8 May for a State visit. On 16 May she went to Chelsea Barracks, where she is seen inspecting the 3rd Battalion Grenadier Guards, of which regiment she was Colonel.

117

THE PRINCESS'S MAY ENGAGEMENTS

Princess Elizabeth had a heavy list of engagements during May, 1951. On the 18th she went to Hastings to hand over to the mayor the title-deeds of its old castle. Next day she visited hospitals in Worthing. On the 21st she attended the Manpower Exhibition, and on the 22nd a Flower Ball at the Savoy Hotel, in aid of the St. Loyes College for Training the Disabled, of which college she is Patron. Here she was presented with a working model of a toy cooking-stove for Prince Charles and a woolly dog for Princess Anne. She is seen (*left*) laughing over the cooking-stove. In the summer of 1951 King George's health began to deteriorate; on 24 May he fell sick with influenza, and on 1 June a slight inflammation of one of his lungs was diagnosed. His illness cast a heavy load of additional duties upon Princess Elizabeth, who had to act for him on a number of official occasions where his presence would otherwise have been anticipated. On 28 May she opened the Exhibition of Industrial Power at Kelvin Hall, Glasgow. On the 29th she visited the Perth Festival of Art to open an Exhibition of Scottish Rural Industries. She is seen (*above*) on the stage of the Perth Theatre, being greeted with music.

A HAPPY FAMILY

Princess Elizabeth and the Duke of Edinburgh are devoted parents and get great joy from their youngsters. These pictures show them in the garden of Clarence House. Princess Anne (*above*) is playfully pressing her fingers against the Duke's lips. In the picture below they are seated on the lawn, and Prince Charles is studying in some perplexity the gay self-confidence of his little sister, to the amusement of his parents.

PRINCESS MARGARET'S TWENTY-FIRST BIRTHDAY

At the end of July, 1951, King George VI was allowed by his doctors to move about quietly, and on 2 August the Royal Family travelled up to Balmoral for a summer holiday. This family group was taken in the grounds of Balmoral Castle on 21 August, Princess Margaret's twenty-first birthday. As the Princess had been born in Scotland it was appropriate that she should be there to celebrate her coming-of-age, but festivities were restricted to a few friends.

ENTERTAINING A CANADIAN SCOT

When holidaying in Scotland, Princess Elizabeth and the Duke of Edinburgh were happy to use the house at Birkhall, by Balmoral, where they had spent the second half of their honeymoon. The Princess is here seen entertaining Lieutenant-Colonel J. A. Farmer, O.C. the Argyll and Sutherland Highlanders of Canada, while the regimental pipe band played at Birkhall. In the lower picture she is about to introduce Colonel Farmer to Princess Anne. With them is Lieutenant-Colonel Neilson, who commanded the 1st Argylls in Korea.

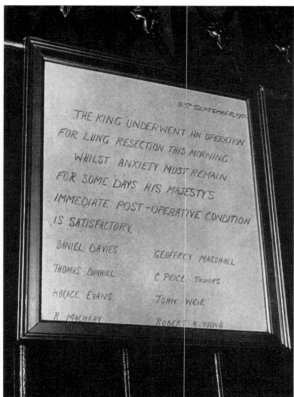

22ND SEPTEMBER 1951

THE KING UNDERWENT AN OPERATION FOR LUNG RESECTION THIS MORNING WHILST ANXIETY MUST REMAIN FOR SOME DAYS HIS MAJESTY'S IMMEDIATE POST-OPERATIVE CONDITION IS SATISFACTORY.

DANIEL DAVIES   GEOFFREY MARSHALL

THOMAS DUNHILL   C. PRICE THOMAS

HORACE EVANS   JOHN WEIR

R MACHRAY   ROBERT R. YOUNG

OPERATION ON KING GEORGE VI

King George's return to health was short-lived. A serious condition had become established in his lung, and in September, 1951, specialists decided that the only hope was an operation to remove the diseased parts. On 23 September an operation for lung resection was successfully performed at Buckingham Palace by Mr. C. Price Thomas, the King's Surgeon. The lower picture shows Princess Elizabeth driving to the Palace on 22 September, while a room there was being prepared for the operation. Above are the anxious crowds that stood silently waiting outside the Palace in the rain, to learn of their King's progress; and the framed bulletin that was hung on the railing. The King made a steady recovery from the operation, and on 7 October the doctors could announce that the post-operative period had passed without complication. But it was widely recognized that, in view of the nature of the disease which had attacked him, his hold on life would be frail.

123

Elaborate preparations had been made for a State visit to Canada by Princess Elizabeth and the Duke of Edinburgh in the autumn of 1951. They were to have sailed from England on 25 September, but King George's illness and operation prevented this. When, however, the doctors were able on 7 October to pronounce the King on the road to recovery, they set off by air, and were able to start their official itinerary at Quebec on 9 October, only a week later than had originally been planned. The Princess and the Duke arrived in Ottawa, the Federal capital, on 10 October; they are seen (*left*) laying a wreath on the Canadian war memorial. In the afternoon Princess Elizabeth (*below*) performed the ceremony of handing over to the National Gallery of Canada the carpet made by Queen Mary. The fruit of many years' work, the carpet is formed of twelve panels of old English flower designs in petit-point embroidery. Queen Mary offered this to the nation in 1951 for sale in America to raise dollars. However, Canada outbid the States for the carpet, which was purchased by the Imperial Order of Daughters of the Empire at a price of 100,000 dollars, for presentation to the Canadian people, after it had been taken on exhibition to a number of cities in the United States.

SCENES ON THE CANADIAN TOUR

During their five weeks' tour of Canada the Prince and Princess visited some fifty communities and saw many of the more famous sights of the Dominion. In the picture (*opposite, top, left*) they are walking through the tunnel to the observation platform below Niagara Falls. The next picture shows the Princess bending over to talk to a little patient when she and Prince Philip visited the new Hospital for Sick Children in Toronto. At this hospital they received a velvet elephant for Princess Anne and a toy power-shovel for Prince Charles. The third picture (*top, right*) shows the mayor of the car-manufacturing town of Windsor, Ontario, demonstrating a toy electric car that was being presented them for Prince Charles. Below, Princess Elizabeth is seen emerging from an Indian Chief's wigwam, during a visit to an assembly of Red Indian tribes at Calgary, Alberta, on 18 October. In the picture on this page Princess Elizabeth and Prince Philip are making their way through a dense crowd to the Legislative Buildings and University of New Brunswick at Fredericton. A massive and enthusiastic welcome was given to the royal couple throughout their tour, in which they traversed the whole of Canada. Princess Elizabeth made a farewell broadcast on 11 November from St. John's, Newfoundland.

A FLYING VISIT TO WASHINGTON

On returning to Montreal from western Canada the Prince and Princess flew to Washington as guests of President Truman. Their plane arrived at Washington airport on Wednesday afternoon, 31 October, and Princess Elizabeth is here seen being greeted by the President and Mrs. Truman as she alights. President Truman made a speech of welcome in which he recalled the visit of her parents to the United States in 1939 and their hospitality to his daughter Margaret when she visited England; while Princess Elizabeth, in her reply, assured him that "free men everywhere look towards the United States with affection and with hope." After this she inspected a guard of honour of a thousand troops drawn up at the airport, while a military band played "God Save the King" and "The Star-Spangled Banner."

A KING'S PRESENT FOR THE WHITE HOUSE

Before leaving Washington on 2 November Princess Elizabeth presented to President Truman, as a gift from King George VI, for the White House which was in course of renovation, an eighteenth-century overmantel of English workmanship, consisting of a pair of candelabra with centre arms of blue-john and finely chased ormolu branches, and a carved gilt landscape mirror with a flower painting above. President Truman, in his reply, paid the warmest of tributes to his royal visitors. On the previous evening he had publicly described Princess Elizabeth as the fairy princess of his childhood's tales come to life, and he now declared that "never before have we had such a wonderful young couple that so completely captured the hearts of all of us!" On all sides they were urged to pay another visit before long.

OFF TO KENYA

On 31 January, 1952, Princess Elizabeth and the Duke of Edinburgh started off from London Airport in the B.O.A.C. Argonaut air-liner *Atalanta* (*left*), which was to take them to Kenya in the first stage of their tour to Australia and New Zealand. Ailing though he was, King George VI came to the airport to see them depart (*below*), accompanied by Queen Elizabeth, Princess Margaret and the Duke of Gloucester. They all knew that the thread of the King's life had worn very thin, but they did not foresee that it was so soon to snap, and the Princess and the Duke went off in high hopes of seeing him again on their return. Within six days, however, they received the news that he had passed away.

THE PRINCESS AND THE DUKE ARRIVE AT NAIROBI

After a safe and uneventful flight the royal tourists reached El Adem in Libya, where they paused to change crews, and then flew on to Nairobi Airport in Kenya, arriving there on 2 February. As they disembarked they were met by the Governor of Kenya, Sir Philip Euen Mitchell. A large crowd had assembled at the airport to welcome them, including the members of the African Advisory Council and representatives of all the various races in the Colony.

KENYA'S WELCOME TO ITS ROYAL GUESTS

Prince, a little African boy, born on the same day as Prince Charles, had been coached to present a bouquet to Princess Elizabeth, but forgot his part and clung to the bouquet, despite coaxing from the Princess and the Mayor of Nairobi (*top, left*). At Nairobi City Hall the Princess and Duke stood on a balcony to salute the cheering crowds (*top, right*). Kenya's wedding present to them was the Royal Lodge at Nyeri, and, after handing over the title-deeds and keys to the Princess (*bottom, left*), the Governor drove with them to the Lodge and is seen (*bottom, right*) helping the Princess to unlock its door, which had jammed.

PRINCESS ELIZABETH INSPECTS THE GUARD OF HONOUR

After landing at Nairobi Airport the Princess formally inspected the Guard of Honour of the Kenya Regiment which was drawn up to receive the royal visitors. The couple spent two days at Government House, Nairobi, and then went on to the Royal Lodge to spend a few days there watching wild life in the African bush. They were resting at the Lodge, after a night of observing big game from a tree-top shelter, when on 6 February a message was telephoned through announcing the death of King George VI. The Duke of Edinburgh broke the news to his wife, who now became Queen Elizabeth II. She bore her bereavement with queenly courage (the report published in some journals that she broke down in tears was quite unfounded) and the two at once made all arrangements to cancel the remainder of their tour and to return immediately to England to assume their new responsibilities.

PROCLAMATION OF QUEEN ELIZABETH II AT WINDSOR

134

Queen Elizabeth II

LESS than a week after Princess Elizabeth and the Duke of Edinburgh had left England for their tour of Australasia, the tragic news of King George's death overtook them in Kenya and brought the young Queen and her husband swiftly home to face the full burden of royal duties and responsibilities.

It was a heavy load for the twenty-five-year-old girl to inherit. Elizabeth II is Queen, not only of the United Kingdom and its Colonies and Dependencies, but of the great self-governing Dominions that ring the world; wide territories of swiftly growing importance whose one official link with Britain and with each other is their common allegiance to the Crown. And while the Queen, as constitutional monarch, does not exercise autocratic rule, her royal functions closely affect the national affairs and social life of her subjects.

Young though she is to bear the weight of these royal responsibilities, Queen Elizabeth has fortunately inherited a far happier position than her queenly pre-decessors. Queen Elizabeth I was only twenty-five when she became ruler of a country rent by bitter religious and political strife, seething with secret conspiracies and open rebellion and assailed by the wealthiest and most formidable Power on the Continent. Queen Victoria came at the age of eighteen to a throne much discredited by the frailties of its previous occupants; and both Elizabeth I and Victoria were single at their accession, while Elizabeth II is supported by a Consort whose ability, character and good sense have won the affectionate confidence of the whole nation.

In Britain today there is no Republican sentiment. The nation knows well the treasure it possesses in its monarchy, which sets at the summit of national life, not money or material power, but honour and courtliness and a lofty standard of behaviour. The Sovereign is not now a tyrant, but the foremost servant of the people, and encourages them by high example to prize honourable conduct and faithful public service above mere wealth. During the past half-century autocratic monarchies have collapsed in every continent, often to be replaced by more sordid standards and harsher forms of tyranny; but the British throne stands firmer than in all its past history, steadied by the character of its occupants and secure in the affection of its subjects.

The Elizabethan and Victorian Ages were the greatest epochs in Britain's past history. That the new Elizabethan Age may surpass them both is the nation's hope.

1

6

2

7

(1) World's first jet air-lin
service began between Lond
and Johannesburg. (2) Outsi
broadcasts on television h
become popular. (3) The hu
Abadan refinery, owned
Britain, remained the focus
the oil dispute, which no
reached deadlock, betwee
Britain and Persia, and led
the breaking-off of diplomat
relations by the latter. (
Guided rockets were bei
developed. (5) The first Briti
atom-bomb was detonated
Monte Bello Island, Austral
(6) Mr. Winston Churchill, t
Prime Minister, addressed Co
gress in Washington. (7) Briti
servicemen were marooned
Greenland for nine days aft
their aircraft had crashed. (
Charlie Chaplin at the Roy
Film Show. (9) Private Spea

3

4

5

8

9

10

11

15

~~m~~an received the V.C. for
~~g~~allantry in Korea. (10) Triple
~~t~~rain crash at Harrow resulted
~~i~~n over a hundred deaths.
(11) Test match at the Oval:
~~E~~ngland *v*. India. (12) The
~~D~~uchess of Kent visited trouble
~~s~~pots in Malaya. (13) Tulyar
~~w~~on the Derby. (14) The
~~F~~lying Enterprise defied salvage
~~e~~fforts and sank after listing
~~f~~or fifteen days. (15) An
~~a~~ircraft of revolutionary design
~~m~~ade its appearance. (16)
~~F~~oxhunter, ridden by Colonel
~~H~~. Llewellyn, won fame at the
~~O~~lympic Games. (17) Oxford
~~w~~on the Boat Race. (18) Disas-
~~t~~rous flood struck Lynmouth,
~~c~~ausing over thirty deaths.
(19) Attempting to set up a
~~w~~ater speed-record on Loch
~~N~~ess, John Cobb was killed
~~w~~hen his jet boat blew up.

12

16

13

17

18

14

19

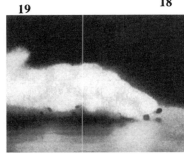

THE QUEEN ARRIVES HOME

On 7 February a group of Privy Councillors, headed by the Prime Minister, Mr. Winston Churchill, assembled at London Airport to receive their new Queen as she arrived back from Nairobi with her husband (*left*). It was a pathetic young figure, clad in black, whom they saw come down the gangway from the plane, followed by the Duke of Edinburgh. But fragile though she seemed, Queen Elizabeth II had all the inner strength of her breed, and accepted without faltering the high duty of sovereignty which now vested in her. Next morning she and the Duke motored down to Sandringham, to join the Queen Mother and the other members of the Royal Family already gathered there, and to put in hand the necessary arrangements for the lying in state and the funeral of King George VI.

WESTMINSTER HALL RECEIVES THE ROYAL DEAD

In accordance with ancient custom, the lying in state of the late King took place in Westminster Hall. On Monday, 11 February, the gun-carriage bearing the royal bier travelled to Wolverton Station, where it was entrained to King's Cross. Under weeping skies it was then drawn through the streets of London, past vast, silent crowds, to Westminster Hall. The Dukes of Edinburgh and Gloucester walked behind it, bare-headed. The cortège was met at the entrance of Westminster Hall by three queens: Queen Elizabeth II, Queen Elizabeth the Queen Mother, and Queen Mary. Members of the King's Company, Grenadier Guards, bore the coffin, draped in the Royal Standard, into the Hall (*right*), and set it there on a catafalque four feet high, to lie in state, with the Imperial State Crown, the Orb and Sceptre, laid upon it. During the next three days an endless stream of mourners filed through the Hall, past this catafalque, to pay in the presence of the royal dead their last tribute of honour and sorrow to a noble King. Each morning at eight o'clock the flow began, and continued without pause into the small hours of the following morning. At times the queue of those waiting their turn was three miles long, and upwards of three hundred thousand passed through Westminster Hall during the lying in state, where about the catafalque officers of the Household troops, Yeomen of the Guard and King's Gentlemen-at-Arms stood guard.

THE FUNERAL PROCESSION ENTERS HYDE PARK

The procession through London of King George's funeral cortège on 15 February, 1952, presented a scene of sombre magnificence. Kings, Presidents and Princes from three continents had assembled to honour his memory and to follow his bier to its last resting place. After them came Commonwealth High Commissioners, Ambassadors and representatives of every foreign State. They passed along streets lined with troops, behind whom an innumerable multitude stood watching through the chill of a wintry day. From Piccadilly the cortège turned into Hyde Park (*above*), where the coffin on its gun-carriage, drawn by a naval gun-crew, passed through the central gateway of Hyde Park Corner, while the Grenadiers of the bearer party divided right and left through the side arches. From the Park the procession wound its way on to Paddington Station, where it entrained for the burial at Windsor.

AT ST. GEORGE'S CHAPEL, WINDSOR CASTLE

In pale winter sunlight the gun-carriage drew up before the steps of St. George's Chapel, just after two o'clock. As the bearer party lifted the coffin and bore it in through the West Door, King George, the Sailor King, was piped home to his last rest with the thin wail of bosuns' pipes. Before the coffin went the Earl Marshal, the Lord Chamberlain and the Lord Steward. Behind followed the Queen and Queen Mother, Princess Margaret and the Princess Royal. The four Royal Dukes came after, and the royal mourners from many lands. There, beneath the exquisite fan-vaulting of the Royal Chapel, the Archbishop of Canterbury pronounced the familiar words of committal, and the coffin was lowered into its vault.

EARLY PUBLIC ENGAGEMENTS

The first public engagement undertaken by Queen Elizabeth II after her accession was her attendance, carrying an Easter bouquet, at the annual Maundy service that is held on the Thursday preceding Good Friday (*above, left*). In medieval times at this service the Sovereign washed the feet of pilgrims and presented them with small doles; but the washing was later remitted to the Lord High Almoner, and two centuries ago was abandoned. The doles have become payments of small silver coins, specially struck for the occasion, and given to a number of elderly poor. On 21 April the Queen reviewed the Grenadier Guards at Windsor Castle on her twenty-sixth birthday, for the first ceremonial parade of her reign (*below, left*). The jewelled brooch she wore had been presented to her by the regiment when she became its Colonel in 1942. On 20 May she went with the Duke of Edinburgh to the Chelsea Flower Show (*above, right*) and spent some time there admiring the great variety of the plants being exhibited.

142

FIRST MEETING OF CORONATION COMMISSION

After the funeral of King George VI was concluded the most important personal problem for Queen Elizabeth was that of the date and arrangements for her Coronation. In olden times no monarch could lay claim to any kingly authority until he had been crowned, and his accession only dated from that ceremony. Saxon kings were often crowned at Kingston-on-Thames, on the King's Stone, but from the time of Edward I English kings have been crowned at Westminster, seated on a throne containing the Holy Stone of Scone, traditionally alleged to be the stone which Jacob used for a pillow at Bethel. It was the Coronation Stone of Scottish kings until Edward I captured it and brought it south. A mystic aura of sacramental symbolism surrounds the ceremony at which the person chosen and approved by the nation is crowned and anointed as its Sovereign. About the procedure at Coronations a

network of old customs has been woven through the centuries, and numbers of people can claim the right to perform traditional duties and services on the occasion. Soon after her accession Queen Elizabeth appointed a Coronation Commission to make arrangements for the ceremony, and announced that 2 June, 1953, had been fixed for its date. The Duke of Edinburgh was named Chairman of the Commission, which contained thirty-six other members. These included the Archbishop of Canterbury, the Lord Chancellor, Prime Minister and eighteen of the principal figures of State and Court in the United Kingdom, and fifteen representatives of the Dominions. The Earl Marshal was appointed Deputy-Chairman. The Earl Marshal is responsible for superintending the arrangements of royal processions and similar state functions. The hereditary holder of this office is the Duke of Norfolk, who was photographed with the Duke of Edinburgh on 5 May, 1952, when the first meeting of the Coronation Commission was held at St. James's Palace.

The first ceremonial Trooping the Colour during the new reign was held on 5 June, and Queen Elizabeth II presided at this ceremony and took the salute. She can be seen above, to the right, inspecting the parade of Guards. She rode the police horse, Winston, and wore the tunic of a Colonel-in-Chief of the Scots Guards; in her tricorne hat was a silver badge of their emblem, presented to her the day before. Queen Elizabeth the Queen Mother, Princess

144

TROOPING THE COLOUR

Margaret, the Princess Royal, the Duchesses of Gloucester and Kent and other members of the Royal Family watched the parade from the Horse Guards building. The Trooping the Colour is a magnificent spectacle of elaborate and complicated drill and military evolutions, faultlessly executed by large bodies of troops simultaneously, and is quite unrivalled as an example of efficient drill. It is held every year on the Horse Guards Parade ground.

PROCLAIMING THE CORONATION

The Proclamation "Declaring Her Majesty's Pleasure touching Her Royal Coronation and the Solemnity thereof" was read on 7 June, 1952, at the traditional four places in London: St. James's Palace, Charing Cross, Chancery Lane and the Royal Exchange. When the cavalcade reached Temple Bar it was challenged according to custom by the City Marshal (*above*). He escorted Rouge Dragon, the Pursuivant, to the Lord Mayor to present the Order in Council, whereupon the Lord Mayor gave permission for the barrier to be thrown back, the procession entered the City and the Royal Proclamation was read at this point by Norroy and Ulster King of Arms. Then the procession swept on to the Royal Exchange.

THE QUEEN OPENS ROYAL ASCOT

To mark the opening of the Royal Ascot race-meeting on 17 June, 1952, Queen Elizabeth II and her guests drove down in open carriages from the Golden Gates along the course to the Royal Enclosure. In the first carriage were the Queen, the Duke of Edinburgh and the Duke of Beaufort (with back to camera). The weather turned fine and warm, but apart from Her Majesty few of the fashionable assembly risked wearing light-coloured summer frocks. The Ascot race-meetings were founded by Queen Anne, after whom the first race of the opening day is named the Queen Anne Stakes. The Queen had a colt, Choir Boy, running in this race, but to the general regret he was unplaced; the winner was Southborne.

QUEEN ELIZABETH VISITS EDINBURGH

The Queen has a special hold upon the loyal affection of the Scottish people, because through her mother she is more Scottish by blood than any British monarch for the past three hundred years. A great crowd of eager people thronged the road when, during her visit to Edinburgh, the Queen was crossing from Acheson House on 25 June to visit the Canongate Kirk.

HOLYROODHOUSE GARDEN PARTY

In the latter part of June Queen Elizabeth II was in residence at the Palace of Holyrood in Edinburgh. On 27 June she gave a garden party there at which she spent more than an hour and a half walking among her seven thousand guests, some of whom were personally presented to her by Lord Mathers (*left*). It was a hot day, and in the evening, after dinner, she sat at an open window and watched the Cameron Highlanders' Pipe Band playing below.

THE ARCHERS' TRIBUTE

On 26 June the Queen was formally presented by the Duke of Buccleugh, Captain-General of the Royal Company of Archers, with a brooch in the form of three crossed arrows (*right*). The Company, which was formed in 1676 by an Act of the Privy Council of Scotland, acts as the Sovereign's Bodyguard for Scotland, in the same way as the Gentlemen-at-Arms do in England. It holds its rights and privileges of the Crown for the payment of a pair of barbed arrows.

149

BRITISH NORTH GREENLAND EXPEDITION

Queen Elizabeth II flew from Scotland on 1 July to visit the members of the British North Greenland Expedition before they sailed for the Arctic in the Norwegian sealer, S.S. *Tottan*, to carry out meteorological and geographical researches. The Queen attended a short service conducted by the Bishop of Portsmouth on the sealer while she lay at her moorings beside Tower Pier, London. Although it was the hottest day of the year—in London the temperature reached 90 deg.—the crew donned their arctic clothing for the Queen's visit.

A VISIT TO THE CHILDREN'S HOSPITAL

Queen Elizabeth paid an informal visit to The Great Ormond Street Hospital for Sick Children in the afternoon of 23 July, and young patients and their nurses crowded the balconies to bid her farewell as she left. While at the hospital she renewed acquaintance with Sister Turner, who had nursed her at Sandringham when she had measles, and also with Sister Hartington, who had similarly nursed Princess Margaret. The Queen stopped to speak to a number of the little patients, who thrust their dolls and toys aside while they greeted her.

THE QUEEN OPENS HER FIRST PARLIAMENT

On 4 November Queen Elizabeth II formally opened the first new parliamentary session of her reign, and delivered her first Speech from the Throne. It was indeed the first to be made by a reigning Queen during the present century. The ceremony was conducted in a setting of that brilliant pageantry at which the British nation excels. The royal procession to the Palace of St. Stephen was headed and completed by escorts of the Household Cavalry, and the route was lined by troops of the Household Brigade. The crown was taken beforehand to Westminster from St. James's Palace in a royal coach, guarded by an escort of Household Cavalry. A salute of forty-one guns was fired when Her Majesty reached the Houses of Parliament, where she was received at the Victoria Tower by the chief officers of State. Then a procession was formed, headed by pursuivants and heralds, and moved up the staircase to the Robing Room; Lord Alexander, the Minister of Defence, carried the Sword of State before Queen Elizabeth, who was conducted by the Duke of Edinburgh. In the Robing Room she donned the parliamentary robe which Queen Victoria had worn on these occasions, and then passed through the Royal Gallery (*right*) to the Parliament Chamber. The Sword of State preceded her, accompanied now by the Cap of Maintenance, borne by Lord Swinton, and the Imperial Crown, borne by Lord Salisbury, on the left and right. She occupied the Throne, and the Duke of Edinburgh sat on a chair placed beside her, in conformity with the precedent Queen Victoria had established for the Prince Consort. The Speech, which she read in her firm, clear voice, set out, as usual, the Government's policy for the new session.

PROCESSION THROUGH THE ROYAL GALLERY OF THE HOUSE OF LORDS

153

STONE-LAYING FOR THE NEW LLOYD'S BUILDING

Queen Elizabeth II, accompanied by the Duke of Edinburgh, was received by the Lord Mayor and his wife (*left*) when she visited Lloyd's premises in the City on 6 November to lay the foundation stone of a new building the underwriters are erecting on a bombed site. It had originally been planned for her father, King George VI, to lay this stone a year earlier. The trowel, mallet and level used were those with which King George V had laid the foundation stone of the present impressive Lloyd's building.

THE QUEEN INSPECTS HER NEW STAMPS

Much careful thought went to the selection of designs for the new postage stamps bearing the portrait of Her Majesty. On 10 November Queen Elizabeth visited the printing works of Messrs. Harrison & Sons at High Wycombe, to see the new 2½d. and 1½d. stamps. She watched Mrs. Irene Dean carefully examining the printed sheets (*right*) as they came off the machine. Miss Enid Marx and Mr. C. F. Ward, who designed respectively the 1½d. and 2½d. stamps, were presented to Her Majesty.

154

PRINCE CHARLES IS FOUR YEARS OLD

This picture of Prince Charles showing his mother a glove-puppet was taken specially, in the grounds of Balmoral, a few days before he celebrated his fourth birthday on 14 November, 1952.

THE CORONATION ROUTE

The plan announced on 21 July, 1952, proposed to take the Coronation procession along Whitehall, both going to and returning from Westminster Abbey; but this elimination of any passage along the Victoria Embankment, where on the last occasion some thirty-seven thousand school-children had assembled, caused so much disappointment that the matter was reconsidered by the Coronation Commission, and on 8 December the Earl Marshal announced the Queen's approval of an altered route to the Abbey (*shown on the following pages*), via Northumberland Avenue, the Victoria Embankment and Bridge Street, which would enable some thousands of children to see the Queen on her way to her Coronation. Arrangements were made accordingly for thirty thousand pupils from schools of Greater London to line both sides of the Embankment on specially provided stands. It was further announced that television of the ceremony within the Abbey had also been considered, and the televising of parts of the service—the Recognition, Crowning and Homage—had been approved.

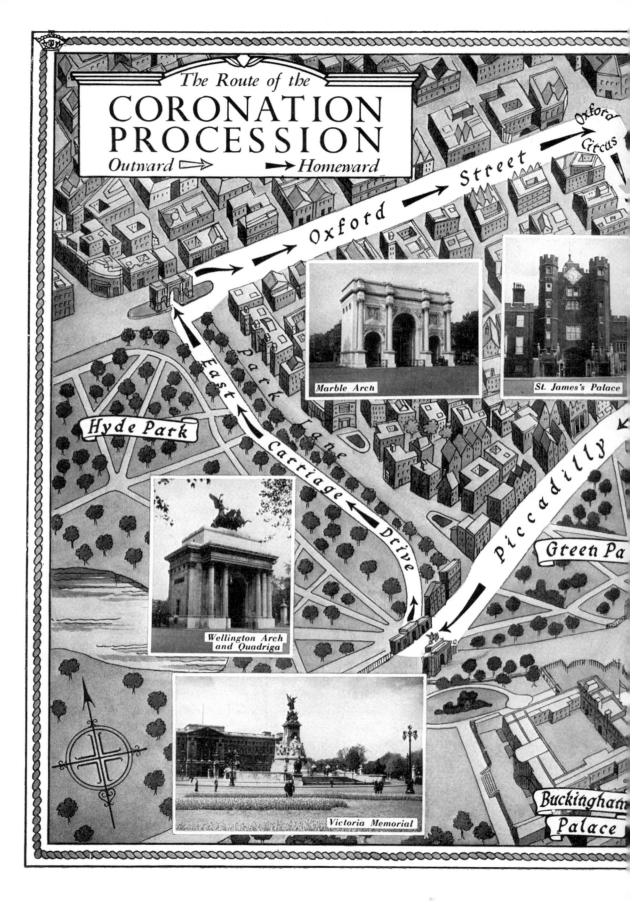

The Route of the
CORONATION PROCESSION
Outward ⇨ ➤ Homeward

Oxford Street

Oxford Circus

Marble Arch

St. James's Palace

Hyde Park

East

Park Lane

Carriage

Drive

Piccadilly

Green Pa[rk]

Wellington Arch
and Quadriga

Victoria Memorial

Buckingham
Palace

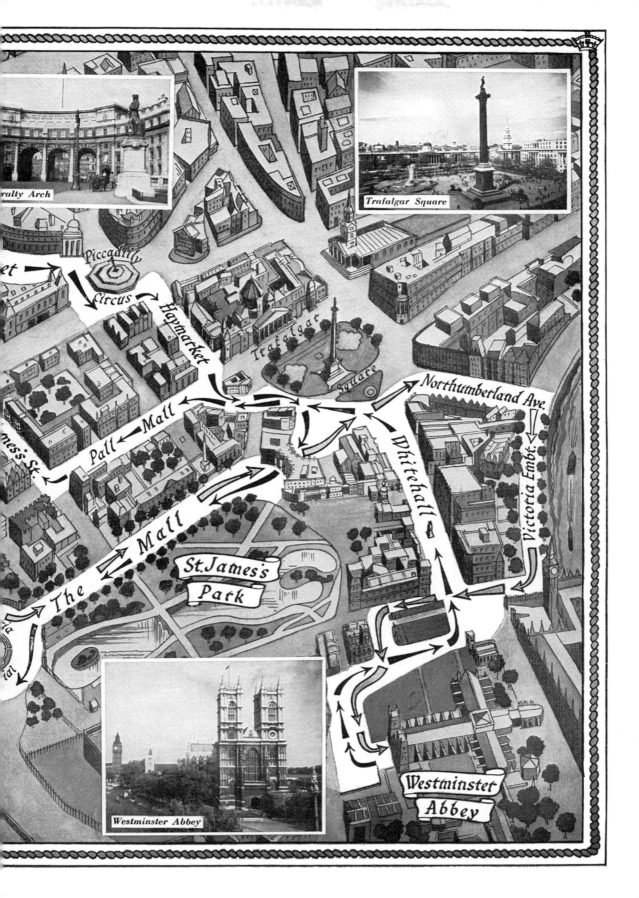

Admiralty Arch

Trafalgar Square

Piccadilly Circus

Haymarket

Trafalgar Square

Northumberland Ave.

Pall Mall

Mall

James's St.

The Mall

St. James's Park

Whitehall

Victoria Embt.

Westminster Abbey

Westminster Abbey

HER MAJESTY AT THE MICROPHONE, CHRISTMAS, 1952

The Queen's Christmas Message

EACH Christmas, at this time, my beloved father broadcast a message to his people in all parts of the world. Today I am doing this to you, who are now my people. As he used to do, I am speaking to you from my own home, where I am spending Christmas with my family: and let me say at once how I hope that your children are enjoying themselves as much as mine are on a day which is especially the children's festival, kept in honour of the Child born at Bethlehem nearly two thousand years ago.

Most of you to whom I am speaking will be in your own homes, but I have a special thought for those who are serving their country in distant lands far from their families. . . . I give you my affectionate greetings, with every good wish for Christmas and the New Year. At Christmas our thoughts are always full of our homes and our families. This is the day when members of the same family try to come together, or if separated by distance or events meet in spirit and affection by exchanging greetings.

But we belong, you and I, to a far larger family. We belong, all of us, to the British Commonwealth and Empire, that immense union of nations, with their homes set in all the four corners of the earth. Like our own families, it can be a great power for good—a force which I believe can be of immeasurable benefit to all humanity. My father and my grandfather before him worked all their lives to unite our peoples ever more closely, and to maintain its ideals which were so near to their hearts. I shall strive to carry on their work. . . . Many grave problems and difficulties confront us all, but with a new faith in the old and splendid beliefs given us by our forefathers, and the strength to venture beyond the safeties of the past, I know we shall be worthy of our duty. . . .

On this broad foundation let us set out to build a truer knowledge of ourselves and our fellow men, to work for tolerance and understanding among the nations, and to use the tremendous forces of science and learning for the betterment of man's lot upon this earth. If we can do these three things with courage, with generosity and with humility, then surely we shall achieve that "peace on earth, good will toward men" which is the eternal message of Christmas, and the desire of us all.

*Extracts from Her Majesty's
broadcast from Sandringham,
25 December, 1952*

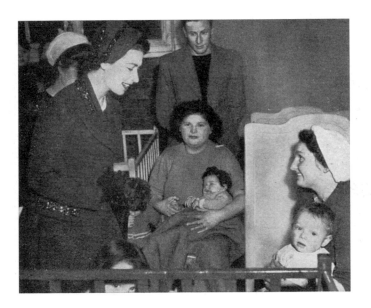

WITH FLOOD VICTIMS

The Queen was at Sandringham when, on 31 January–1 February, Britain's worst natural disaster for over two centuries struck the East Coast. The sea burst inland, flooding huge areas, causing over three hundred deaths and enormous damage. The Queen immediately went to see for herself the effect of the calamity. On 2 February she visited devastated areas in Norfolk and eleven days later she made an extensive tour of Thames Estuary flood areas, including a visit to mothers and children in an emergency rest centre at Tilbury.

THE QUEEN AT THE ROYAL ACADEMY

"Kings and Queens A.D. 653–1953" was the title of an exhibition arranged by the Royal Academy at Burlington House, London, in March. The Queen lent a number of pictures from the royal collections, including Winterhalter's painting of Queen Victoria, the Prince Consort, and their children, which interested the Queen during a visit to the exhibition.

DEATH OF QUEEN MARY

With the time of the Coronation rapidly approaching, enthusiastic preparations were under way, but the month of March brought sorrow once again to the Royal Family and to the nation. An announcement on 2 March revealed that Queen Mary was suffering from a recurrence of gastric trouble, and anxious eyes turned to read the medical bulletins from Marlborough House. After a brief illness Queen Mary died peacefully in her sleep in the night of 24 March. Her thoughtfulness for others, and the devotion to duty which she displayed throughout her life, had earned her the deep affection of the British people; it was characteristic that her last-expressed wish should be that there must be no postponement of the Coronation. On 29 March, through streets lined with sorrowing crowds, the gun-carriage bearing Queen Mary's coffin made its sad journey to Westminster Hall for the lying-in-state. In the procession (*above*) were the four Royal Dukes of Edinburgh, Windsor, Gloucester and Kent. The royal coffin was conveyed privately by car to St. George's Chapel, Windsor, for the burial service on 31 March. Surmounting Queen Mary's Standard was the wreath of spring flowers from Her Majesty the Queen, with the inscription "In loving memory from her devoted Lilibet and Philip." The final ceremony was simple and moving. At its conclusion the Queen looked once more into the royal vault and made her last curtsey to her grandmother. The Court went into mourning for one month, but in the words of the Prime Minister's tribute, broadcast on 25 March, "Queen Mary will long live mellow and gracious in all our memories."

PAGEANTRY AT WINDSOR

Against the impressive background of historic Windsor Castle Her Majesty the Queen took part on 28 April in a ceremony which was rich in colour and tradition. For the first time for many years the two regiments of Household Cavalry—the Life Guards and the Royal Horse Guards—received new Standards from their Sovereign. The old colours were trooped and marched off to the accompaniment of "Auld Lang Syne" played by massed bands resplendent in gold State dress. After the playing of the National Anthem the Queen reviewed the troops.

FINAL PREPARATIONS

In the few weeks preceding the day of her Coronation the Queen was required to carry out an increasingly heavy programme of official duties. Nevertheless, she brought to every task the same unflagging energy and evident enjoyment that had endeared her to the people in the years before her accession to the Throne. The Queen is seen (*right*) arriving on 27 May for her fifth rehearsal at Westminster Abbey. With Her Majesty is the Earl Marshal the Duke of Norfolk, whose organizing ability ensured that final preparations for 2 June were well in hand at an early date. On the same day Queen Elizabeth attended the Coronation luncheon of the Commonwealth Parliamentary Association, which was held in Westminster Hall. Among the representatives of the peoples of the Commonwealth on this notable occasion were the Prime Ministers of Canada, Australia and New Zealand; Sir Winston Churchill, Prime Minister of Great Britain, is seen proposing a vote of thanks to Her Majesty.

TAKEN AT BUCKINGHAM PALACE, 2 JUNE, 1953

164

The Coronation
of Queen Elizabeth II

"GOD SAVE THE QUEEN." With "loud and repeated shouts" the great congregation numbering over seven thousand filled the ancient Abbey of Westminster with the sound of acclamation. As they gave voice so did the trumpets in a royal fanfare and in the west towers the bells of the Abbey rang out. In the distance at the Tower of London and nearer at St. James's Park the "great guns" fired the opening rounds of a royal salute.

So, on 2 June, 1953, was the exact moment of crowning of Her Majesty Queen Elizabeth II marked—the climax of a ceremony of unparalleled splendour and dignity.

It is difficult to separate the many facets which contributed to the total impression of this unforgettable day—the hundreds of thousands of spectators, many of them after hours of waiting, who crowded the route of the Coronation procession; the brilliance of the decorations; the precision and pageantry of the marching troops and the music of their bands; the beauty of the Coronation Service itself; or the vision of a young Queen in a golden coach, receiving the cheers of her people.

But perhaps the strongest impression left by the Coronation was that this event, taking place within the narrow confines of the City of Westminster, was not only a national event but a great Commonwealth event, and that all those countries which make up the Commonwealth were themselves celebrating the Coronation on the same day. For the first time had been crowned a Sovereign with the title "Head of the Commonwealth" as well as that of Queen of many of its member nations—"a young Queen for a young Commonwealth," to quote an Australian minister a few days before the event. Not that all this was just an idea. The processions and the Coronation Service had ample evidence of it. Eleven Prime Ministers rode in the procession—all heads of Governments either owing allegiance to Her Majesty or recognizing in her the bond which unites the Commonwealth.

The great procession from the Abbey after the ceremony emphasized the diversity of race, colour and culture of the Commonwealth family. There were police from the Solomon Islands, the Windward Islands and Trinidad, servicemen from Hong Kong,

Malaya, Aden, Barbados, British Guiana, the Leeward and Falkland Islands, Gibraltar, Fiji, Somaliland, Kenya and Mauritius—to mention at random some of the Colonial territories, names scattered over the whole globe, each conjuring up a romantic vision of its own. And then there were the contingents from the great self-governing dominions, now including Pakistan and Ceylon which had achieved this new status since the Queen's father was crowned sixteen years ago.

All these Peoples the Queen had, at the beginning of the Coronation Service, solemnly promised and sworn to govern "according to their respective laws and customs"; and when she was later invested with the items of the Regalia, these included, for the first time since the Coronation of Edward VI over four centuries ago, the Armills or "bracelets of sincerity and wisdom." But this time they were new Armills, presented, as appropriate, by the Governments of the Commonwealth.

On the morning of the Coronation the waiting crowds had their first taste of pageantry with the arrival at the Abbey of the Lord Mayor of London. His procession was followed by that of the Speaker of the House of Commons (in his ancient coach that was once a royal state coach), by certain members of the Royal Family in motor-cars, the royal and other representatives of foreign states, the procession of Colonial rulers led by the Queen of Tonga's carriage, the Prime Ministers led by Sir Winston Churchill, the Princes and Princesses of the Blood Royal, Queen Elizabeth the Queen Mother and Princess Margaret, and last of all the Queen herself with the Duke of Edinburgh seated beside her in the state coach, and escorted by the Household Cavalry, the chiefs of her fighting forces, her bargemaster and watermen and many another whose duty it was to attend her on this great occasion.

Inside the annexe built at the west door of the Abbey the procession—among the most brilliant spectacles to be seen anywhere in the world—formed up for its slow and dignified journey to the theatre in front of the altar. Here the solemn rites, described in detail earlier in this book, were performed.

And then the grand procession from all parts of the Commonwealth moved between five miles of cheering crowds back to the Palace, in time for the Queen to be on the balcony for the fly-past by the Royal Air Force. So ended the great pageant of the Coronation, but the day did not end before the Queen, a small figure on the distant balcony of Buckingham Palace, had several times appeared to acknowledge the insistent cheers of the multitude. And at last at the touch of a switch the Queen turned the centre of London into a fairy city as the Coronation lights cascaded into brilliance.

166

THE QUEEN MOTHER AND PRINCESS MARGARET ON THE WAY TO THE ABBEY

The Queen Mother and Princess Margaret travelled from Clarence House to the Abbey in the Irish State Coach, escorted by detachments of the Household Cavalry. The Queen Mother, poised and gracious, looked resplendent in her gold and white gown and purple robe; and Princess Margaret, tiara on head, was a small, enchanting figure in embroidered satin.

THE QUEEN LEAVING
BUCKINGHAM PALACE

A night of cold and drizzle could not quench the enthusiasm of the great crowds in the Mall. At 3.30 a.m. they were already twelve deep with every minute bringing fresh arrivals. Tension mounted as the processions began to flow along the Mall towards Admiralty Arch. Just before ten thirty the State Coach emerged from the Palace gates (*above*) and one of the great moments of a great day had arrived. Prince Charles (*left*), at one of the Palace windows, was an interested spectator.

168

THE QUEEN RIDING TO HER CROWNING

The Queen, seated beside the Duke of Edinburgh in the Royal State Coach, was a radiant figure. Relaxed and serene, she happily acknowledged the tremendous reception of her people.

ROYAL PROCESSION IN THE MALL

The State Coach moves along the crowded Mall, which has been lined by the Brigade of Guards since eight o'clock in the morning. In front of Her Majesty rides the Second Division, Sovereign's Escort, and behind her the personal and service aides-de-camp, equerries, grooms, and the Third and Fourth Division Sovereign's Escort.

NEARING THE ABBEY

As the golden State Coach made its way along the Victoria Embankment (*below*), the Queen received what was perhaps her greatest ovation of the day—from the thirty-one thousand school-children lining this part of the route. Their cheering doubled and redoubled in volume as each new sight moved into view, finally reaching a veritable crescendo with the approach of the Queen. The Duke of Gloucester and Earl Mountbatten of Burma (*right*), personal aides-de-camp to the Queen, ride at a short distance behind the State Coach.

ARRIVAL AT WESTMINSTER ABBEY

The stands in St. Margaret's churchyard, Parliament Square, and on the site of the new Colonial Office, had been packed since six o'clock in the morning. From nine o'clock onwards the crowds there gathered had seen the various processions approach Westminster Abbey and make their way to the annexe at the western door. Now the climax was reached with the arrival of the Queen's coach at the end of its journey (*above*). The Earl Marshal stands on the steps of the annexe to receive Her Majesty. (*Left*) The Queen has descended from her coach and is about to enter the annexe.

172

THE QUEEN'S PROCESSION MOVES UP THE NAVE OF THE ABBEY

The great procession preceding the Queen into the Abbey was led by the Dean and Preben-
daries of Westminster, and representatives of the Church of Scotland and of the Free Churches.
Next came the officers of the knighthood and the standards of the Commonwealth countries
borne by the High Commissioners; the Union Standard; the Standard of Wales; the Standards
of the quarterings of the Royal Arms; and the Royal Standard, borne by Lord Montgomery
of Alamein. Behind Lord Montgomery came the four Knights of the Garter who were to
hold the canopy over the Queen during her anointing; the Prime Ministers of the Commonwealth States; the Archbishops of York and Canterbury; and the Duke of Edinburgh. Immediately preceding the Queen were the bearers of her Regalia. The Queen was escorted by
the Bishops of Durham and of Bath and Wells (*above*), her crimson train being held by six
Maids of Honour; and behind her walked the Mistress of the Robes.

173

AT THE CHAIR OF ESTATE

Proceeding to the Chair of Estate, the Queen knelt in prayer while the various items of the Regalia were handed by their bearers to the Archbishop of Canterbury—who in turn handed them to the Dean of Westminster to place upon the altar. There followed the Recognition. With four of the Secular Lords, the Archbishop of Canterbury faced each side of the square theatre in turn, saying: "Sirs, I here present unto you Queen Elizabeth, your undoubted Queen: Wherefore all you who are come this day to do your homage and service, Are you willing to do the same?" Having been acclaimed from all sides, the Queen took the Oath by which she promised to govern all her peoples according to their respective laws and customs, to cause law and justice in mercy to be executed in all her judgements, and to maintain in the United Kingdom the Protestant reformed religion. The presentation of the Bible completed the preliminaries to the Anointing. Above, the Queen is seen seated on the Chair of Estate.

BEFORE THE ANOINTING

The Anointing forms part of the Communion Service and is the spiritual climax of the Coronation. While the choir sang Handel's "Zadok the Priest" the Queen divested herself of her great train and her jewelry. Arrayed now in a simple white robe, she followed the Sword of State to King Edward's Chair. Four Knights of the Garter held a canopy of cloth-of-gold over her (*above*). The Archbishop of Canterbury, followed by the Dean of Westminster bearing the Ampulla and Spoon, advanced towards her. Dipping his thumb in the oil which the Dean had poured into the Spoon, the Archbishop anointed the Queen upon hands, breast and head "as kings, priests and prophets were anointed."

PRINCE CHARLES WATCHES HIS MOTHER

Prince Charles was an interested spectator of the ceremony. Taken by back streets to a side door of the Abbey, he slipped into the Royal Box between the Queen Mother and Princess Margaret just before the Anointing. Almost immediately he was plying his grandmother and aunt with questions. He witnessed the Crowning and saw his father, the Duke of Edinburgh, kneel in homage before the Queen. At the completion of the Homage he was led unobtrusively away.

175

THE PRESENTATION OF THE REGALIA

The Anointing over, the Queen could now be invested with the emblems of temporal authority. The Mistress of the Robes removed the simple white dress, and the Dean of Westminster put upon her the Colobium Sindonis and the golden Supertunica. The spurs of St. George were brought to her by the Lord Great Chamberlain so that she might touch them. Lord Salisbury, who had hitherto been carrying the great Sword of State, now exchanged it for the smaller jewelled sword, which the Archbishop delivered into the hands of the Queen. Rising from King Edward's Chair, the Queen advanced to the Altar (*above*) to surrender the sword— a symbol of her surrender of temporal power to God. Next, the Armills were fastened upon her wrists as "symbols and pledges of that bond which unites you with your peoples," and the gorgeous stole and robe royal were placed upon her. The Queen was now ready to receive the greater symbols. In turn were brought to her the Orb; the Ring, placed on her finger by the Archbishop; and the Sceptre with the Cross and the Rod with the Dove, always presented together as a sign that justice and mercy must never be separated. The culminating act of the crowning ceremony was at hand. The Archbishop lifted the great Crown of St. Edward from its cushion, and placed it upon the Queen's head. Immediately the congregation cried: "God Save the Queen." The peers and peeresses put on their coronets and the Kings of Arms their crowns; fanfares of trumpets pealed out; and the Tower guns thundered their salute.

THE QUEEN IS CROWNED

THE QUEEN ENTHRONED

After the Coronation the Enthronement. The bearers of the three swords of justice—the Sword of Spiritual Justice, the Sword of Temporal Justice, and Curtana, Sword of Mercy—took up positions behind the Throne; and the Lords, hitherto grouped around King Edward's Chair, formed a semicircle round the steps. The Queen rose and, with the Bishops of Durham and of Bath and Wells, moved from the Chair and slowly ascended the five steps of the Throne. She was now "lifted" into her symbolic seat of governance by Church and State in the persons of the Archbishop of Canterbury and the Duke of Norfolk. The ministration of the crowning rite was over. Seated in the Throne (*above*) and invested with all the temporal power of the State, the Queen was ready to receive her Homage. (*Left*) A general view of the scene after the Queen had been crowned (looking from above the altar towards the west door of the Abbey).

The Archbishop of Canterbury was the first to kneel in fealty to the Queen of the Realm and Defender of the Faith. With him knelt also in their places the bishops. The Queen's consort, the Duke of Edinburgh, was the first of the temporal peers to do homage. Placing his coronet on the cushion held by one of the pages of the Earl Marshal, he mounted the steps of the Throne and knelt before the Queen. Then, laying his hands in hers, he pronounced the words of the Homage (*below*). Rising, he kissed the Queen's cheek, touched the Crown in token that he would support it with all his power, resumed his coronet and returned to his place. In like manner the Duke of Gloucester and the Duke of Kent did their homage; and afterwards the senior peer of each degree, the Duke of Norfolk, the Marquess of Huntly, the Earl of Shrewsbury, Viscount Arbuthnot, and Lord Mowbray, performed his homage, while with each the peers of the same degree knelt in their places and repeated with him the words.

THE QUEEN'S PROCESSION PASSES DOWN THE ABBEY NAVE

The Homage over, the Communion Service was resumed. The Queen moved slowly to the altar on reaching which she delivered her Crown, Sceptre and Rod into the waiting hands and knelt down. At the end of the hymn "All people that on earth do dwell," the Queen offered the Bread and Wine for the Communion. Then having made her oblation the Queen went to her faldstool; the Duke of Edinburgh, coming at the same time to his, took off his coronet. They knelt down together to receive the Communion. The Queen then returned to her Throne. A Benediction followed and the Queen's Coronation was ended. Preceded by the four swords, she passed into St. Edward's Chapel to re-emerge after a short recess bearing the Sceptre and Orb and wearing for the first time the Imperial Crown. The Queen's procession moved in state through the choir and nave of the Abbey (*above*) to the west door.

181

LEAVING THE ANNEXE

The Queen, Orb in left hand and Sceptre in right hand, steps out of the annexe into the sight of the crowds gathered in the stand in Broad Sanctuary. A fanfare of trumpets sound and the people cheer. Awaiting her is the golden coach in which she is to make her triumphal return to Buckingham Palace through the loyal millions lining the route.

DOMINION AND COLONIAL TROOPS IN THE RETURN PROCESSION

As the Queen re-entered her coach outside the Abbey, the head of the procession preceding her triumphal journey through London stood at Stanhope Gate, in Hyde Park, nearly two miles away. This great procession, made up of nearly ten thousand service men and women, comprised contingents of the Armies, Navies, Air Forces and Police of all the self-governing Dominions, as well as representative soldiery of the Colonies, dependencies and protectorates. The head of the procession moved off at 3.15 p.m., those on foot marching ten abreast and those on horseback in sixes. Twenty-seven service bands were interspersed through the procession. The crowds, soaked by pitiless downpours of rain, had lost none of their enthusiasm. They shouted themselves hoarse as wave upon colourful wave of soldiery swept by them. The Colonial contingent, part of which is seen here (*top*, *right*), followed the leading bands and was enthusiastically greeted. The lithe figures of the Pakistanis moved among the Dominion troops (*centre*, *right*), and a special cheer greeted the almost legendary Canadian Mounties (*bottom*, *right*).

183

THE PEOPLE GREET THEIR QUEEN

The long, broad sweep of East Carriage Drive presented marching opportunity second only to that of the Mall, and the troops availed themselves of it to show off their paces. At the Marble Arch the troops had a difficult manoeuvre to perform; they had to split into three columns to pass through the park gates, close partially to pass under the arch, and then wheel sharp right into Oxford Street. The United Kingdom naval contingent is seen (*above*) admirably performing the first part of this manoeuvre. Behind the sailors came the Foot Guards and the Royal Horse Artillery. Then followed the Carriage Procession of Colonial Rulers—the Sultans of Lahej, Selangor, Brunei, Johore, Perak, Zanzibar, Kelentan; and the Queen of Tonga, who won the affection of the crowds by her happy smile and complete disregard of the elements (she rode throughout in an open coach). The colourful uniforms of the mounted escorts from the different Commonwealth countries contrasted with the dark carriages of the Prime Ministers with which they rode. All along the route there was a special cheer for the Queen Mother and Princess Margaret. Then came the mighty procession of the Queen, studded with eminent men; and finally the Queen herself. Even for those who could not see the loveliness of the woman within, the golden coach presented an appearance of floating beauty not quite of this world. (*Right*) The Queen's coach passes through Piccadilly Circus beside the crowds massed round the temporarily caged Eros; and on pages 186–7 it nears the end of its journey as it passes for the third time that day through Trafalgar Square.

RETURN TO THE PALACE

The State Coach passes round the Victoria Memorial just prior to entering the Palace (*below*). The railings are lined by the double ranks of the guards of honour, formed by the Royal Navy, the Irish Guards and the Royal Air Force. The Victoria Memorial had been occupied by service cadets, who remained irrepressibly lively throughout the day. (*Left*) A view of the impeccable ranks of Regiments of the Brigade of Guards as they returned to the Palace along the Mall.

THE SMILING QUEEN

The State Coach was followed into the forecourt of the Palace by the two divisions of the Sovereign's Escort. All eyes tried to follow the coach in the melee of the forecourt, until its final disappearance into the inner courtyard. The Queen was still smiling and showing no signs of strain as she alighted from the coach carrying the Orb and Sceptre.

189

AERIAL SALUTE

Meteor jets of the Royal Air Force fly over Buckingham Palace in salute to the Queen. In view of the poor visibility the original plans for a tightly packed fly-past were modified, and the Meteors and Sabres flew in loose formation with thirty-second intervals between each wave. Seven groups of twenty-four aircraft each took part in the fly-past.

THE QUEEN AND HER FAMILY WAVE TO THE CROWDS

Not for long after the Queen had entered the Palace could the crowds be kept in check. Hardly had the guards of honour at the Palace and the troops who had been lining the route been withdrawn, than the eager crowds started to press against the police cordons, which eventually broke before the strain. The people flooded in their thousands to the Palace railings shouting thunderously for the Queen. Their call was answered sooner than the most sanguine could have expected. At twenty minutes to six the balcony windows opened and the Queen appeared, followed by the Duke of Edinburgh, Prince Charles and Princess Anne. A few moments later they were joined by the six maids of honour, the Queen Mother, Princess Margaret, and other members of the royal family. The Queen waved happily to the crowd, and was vigorously emulated by Prince Charles and Princess Anne. She remained on the balcony for ten minutes while fresh thousands surged forward from the Mall, Constitution Hill and Buckingham Palace Road. This was but the first of a number of appearances she was to make on the balcony during the evening of this very memorable, and very wonderful, day.

INDEX

ACKNOWLEDGEMENTS

The Publishers are indebted to the following for permission to reproduce the illustrations on the pages indicated: the Trustees of the British Museum: pages 24, 25, 27, 28, 44; the National Maritime Museum: page 22; the National Portrait Gallery: pages 29, 31; the Tate Gallery: page 45; and Picture Post Library: pages 21, 32, 33.

The colour-plates (numbered in the order listed on page 5) are from photographs by Karsh of Ottawa (1 and 3); Planet News Ltd. (2 and 7); Central Office of Information (5); Baron (6); A. C. K. Ware (Photographs) Ltd. (8); Marcus Adams (9). The colour-plate of the regalia was specially drawn for this book by H. Doust.

First published in Great Britain by Odhams Press Limited.

This edition published 2006 by Bounty Books,
a division of Octopus Publishing Group Ltd
2–4 Heron Quays, London E14 4JP

Copyright © Octopus Publishing Group Ltd 2006

ISBN-13: 978-0-753714-49-2
ISBN-10: 0-753714-49-3

A CIP catalogue record for this book is available from the British Library. Printed and bound in Slovenia